Harshad Kot

Windows Vista

in
easy steps

Now Fully Updated for
Service Pack 1

In easy steps is an imprint of In Easy Steps Limited
Southfield Road · Southam
Warwickshire CV47 0FB · United Kingdom
www.ineasysteps.com

Second edition

Notice of Liability
Every effort has been made to ensure that this book contains accurate
and current information. However, In Easy Steps Limited and the
author shall not be liable for any loss or damage suffered by readers
as a result of any information contained herein.

Trademarks
Microsoft® and Windows® are registered trademarks of Microsoft
Corporation. All other trademarks are acknowledged as belonging to
their respective companies.

Printed and bound in the United Kingdom

ISBN-13 978-1-84078-366-7
ISBN-10 1-84078-366-4

Contents

8 Email and Windows 127

9 Fonts and Printing 145

10 Networking 159

11 Customize Windows 169

12   Digital Media   193

Reference section: Maintenance   209

Index   233

1 Windows Editions

This chapter explains what Windows is and what's new in this latest version. It will help you identify the edition of Vista that will suit you best, determine if your existing computer will handle Windows Vista and advise any actions needed.

What is Windows?

Windows is an operating system. This is the software that organizes and controls all the components in your computer (both hardware and software) so that they integrate and work efficiently together. All computers need an operating system to function and Windows is the most popular one as it's installed on most of the world's PCs (personal computers).

Don't forget

There were also versions aimed specifically at businesses, including Windows NT, Windows 2000 and Windows 2003, used mainly on server machines, rather than end user computers.

The basic foundation underlying any version of Windows is its "windowing" capability. A window (with a lower-case w) is a rectangular area used to display information or to run a program. Several windows can be opened at the same time to work with multiple applications, so you should be able to dramatically increase your productivity when using your PC.

Microsoft has released many versions of Windows over the years, including:

- Windows 95

- Windows 98 and 98 SE (second edition)

- Windows ME (millennium edition)

- Windows XP (eXPerience)

In Windows XP, Microsoft introduced an edition designed for the consumer (Home Edition) and an edition for the business user (Professional). Windows XP Professional included all the features of Windows XP Home Edition plus enhanced networking, mobile computing, corporate management and security features. There were also specialized releases for the Tablet PC (featuring a pressure sensitive screen that you can write on), the Media Center PC (with TV tuner) and the 64-bit PC (with 64-bit rather than the normal 32-bit processor).

Hot tip

This book covers Windows Vista business and consumer products, catering for many different types of Windows Vista user.

Windows Vista
The latest version of Windows is Windows Vista. This consists of six products - two editions for business, an entry edition for emerging markets and three editions for consumers.

Windows Vista Editions

We'll start with the two Windows Vista business editions:

Windows Vista Business

This is designed for organizations of all sizes, to keep PCs running smoothly and more securely so they are less reliant on dedicated IT support. Features include:

- Windows Aero, the new user interface, that uses transparent glass design, with subtle effects such as dynamic reflections and smooth animations

- Integrated search facilities and new ways to organize files, to help manage large volumes of business documents

- Windows Tablet PC technology providing handwriting recognition for entries from a digital pen or fingertip

Windows Vista Enterprise

This targets large global organizations with highly complex IT infrastructures, adding features such as:

- Windows BitLocker drive encryption to help prevent access to data if a computer is lost or stolen

- Virtual PC Express and other built-in tools that improve application compatibility

- Subsystem for UNIX-based Applications to allow users to run UNIX applications unchanged

Windows Vista Starter

This edition is for beginner PC users in emerging markets, and is a 32-bit operating system for lower-cost computers, intended as an easy-to-use and affordable entry point to Windows Vista. It is limited to three simultaneous applications and/or windows, it provides Internet connectivity but not incoming network communications and it does not support logon passwords or fast user switching. Windows Vista Starter edition is not available in North America or Europe.

Hot tip

All new versions (except the Starter edition) are available for either 32-bit or 64-bit systems.

Hot tip

Windows Vista Starter edition is a subset of the Windows Vista Basic edition (see page 10).

...cont'd

For the consumer or home user, there are three editions offered.

Windows Vista Home Basic

For users who simply want to use the PC to browse the Internet, correspond with friends and family through email or perform basic document creation and editing tasks, in a safe, reliable and productive computing environment. Features include:

- Windows Sidebar and Sidebar Gadgets

- Parental Controls

Windows Vista Home Premium

This allows consumers to take full advantage of digital entertainment options including photos, video, TV, movies, music and games, adding features and enhancements such as:

- The Windows Aero new user interface

- Integrated search facilities, in this case to organize large collections of documents, pictures, movies, videos and music

- Windows Media Center capabilities, to turn the PC into an all-in-one home entertainment center, where users can record and watch TV shows (including high-definition TV)

- Integrated DVD burning and authoring, to burn personal videos, photos and files to video or data DVDs, also create professional-looking DVDs from home movies

- Windows Tablet PC technology is also available in this edition of Windows Vista

Windows Vista Ultimate

This edition has everything, bringing together the entertainment, mobility and business-oriented features available in all the other editions of Windows Vista. This edition will also feature:

- Windows Ultimate Extras - programs, services, tutorials and information available to Ultimate users

If you have the Home Basic edition, the features of the Home Premium and Ultimate editions may be unlocked at any time by purchasing a one-time upgrade license through Windows Anytime Upgrade in the Control Panel.

Windows Vista PC

PCs intended for running Windows vista must match up to the specifications at the desired level. There are two main categories:

Windows Vista Capable

The Windows Vista capable PC will have the minimum supported hardware requirements for running the core Windows Vista features (this excludes the Windows Aero user interface):

- Processor — 800 MHz 32-bit (x86) or 64-bit (x64)
- System Memory — 512 MB
- Graphics — SVGA (800x600)
- Graphics adapter — DirectX9 class
- Graphics memory — 64 MB
- Hard Disk — 20 GB
- Other — CD-ROM drive

Windows Premium Ready

The Windows Premium ready PC will have the hardware requirements to support all the capabilities of Windows Vista, including Windows Aero:

- Processor — 1 GHz 32-bit (x86) or 64-bit (x64)
- System Memory — 1 GB
- Graphics — SVGA (800x600)
- Graphics adapter — Windows Display Driver Model (WDDM)
- Graphics memory — 128 MB
- Hard Disk — 40 GB
- Other — DVD drive

A list of graphics adapter cards that support WDDM can be found at http://www.microsoft.com/technet/windowsvista/evaluate/hardware/entpguid.mspx

If you want to upgrade your existing PC to run Windows Vista, see the Upgrade Advisor (page 12). If you already have the system installed, go on to Starting Windows Vista (page 17).

Don't forget

These are the supported specifications. However, Windows Vista's Basic and Classic interfaces will work with virtually any graphics hardware that supports Windows XP (see page 12).

Hot tip

Additional hardware includes a pointing device such as a mouse, a sound card and speakers. Note that the BitLocker Drive Encryption requires a TPM 1.2 chip or a USB 2.0 flash drive.

Upgrade Advisor

This scans a Windows XP-based PC, to see how well it could run Windows Vista. It creates a report of known system and device compatibility issues, recommends ways to resolve them, and helps choose the best edition of Windows Vista to suit your needs.

1 Go to the www.microsoft.com/windowsvista/ website and click the Windows Vista link asking 'Is your PC ready for Vista?'

2 Click the Download link and select Save to write the installation file onto your hard drive

3 Double-click the Upgrade Advisor file, and follow the prompts to install and start up the program

4 Click Start Scan to begin the analysis of your computer's hardware and software

Feature Review

While the scan is running, the Advisor displays the main features of the four main editions and the two European editions (the N editions, with no Windows Media Player).

Hot tip

There's a review page for each of the editions. You can click the Edition Name buttons to switch between the pages, while the scan is in process.

1 When Upgrade Advisor tells you the scan has completed, click the See Details button to view the results

Hot tip

The Advisor will recommend one of the four editions, based on the current configuration of your computer and will advise the necessary changes, if you want to install a different edition (see page 14).

Report Summary

1 You may find that your computer is unable to run Vista without hardware upgrades (in this case, disk storage)

Don't forget

If you are planning to reinstall your complete system, then the drive can be reformatted during setup and you won't have to worry about the requirement for free disk space.

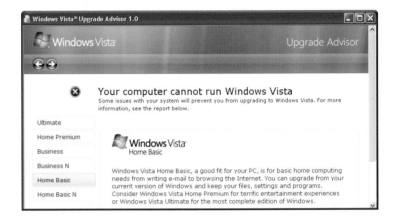

2 Home Basic is recommended because of limited memory and features on the graphics adapter. If you select any other edition, you'll get a warning about the graphics card

3 The Advisor recognizes when the computer meets the basic requirements for Windows Vista

Don't forget

Even when the computer fully meets the memory, processor and graphics card specifications, there may be additional needs, such as a TV tuner for media center operation.

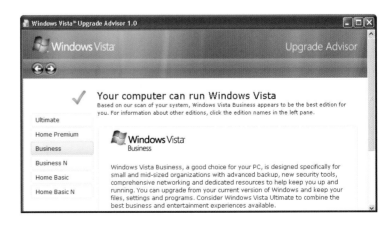

Detailed Results

There is a detailed assessment of the devices and the programs on your computer, plus a task list of the actions that you need to take.

1 For some devices, you need to install the Windows Vista drivers via Windows Update, after upgrading the system

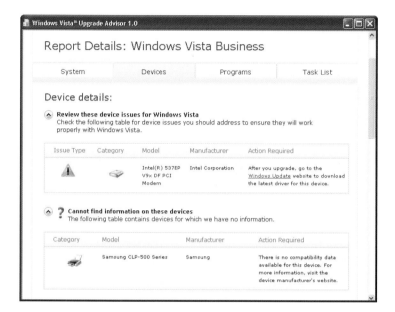

2 There are some devices that the Advisor cannot recognize. For these, you must visit the manufacturer's website

3 The Advisor warns of any program compatibility issues

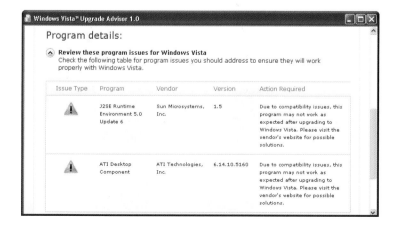

Hot tip

Print or save the full report before exiting the Upgrade Advisor.

Beware

Some devices that are no longer in current production may never receive upgrades to their device drivers.

Don't forget

Run the Upgrade Advisor report again, before you upgrade your system, to see if there have been any changes to the level of support.

Service Pack 1 (SP1)

A year after the launch of Windows Vista, Microsoft introduced Service Pack 1, which included all the updates to that point plus a large number of additional updates. The purpose of SP1 is to improve the reliability, performance, and security of Windows Vista. SP1 also adds support for new technologies and standards. However, it does not extend to new operating system features.

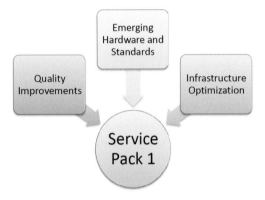

Even though there are no substantive changes in function, SP1 installation is a major effort that may take an hour or more, and involve several restarts. See page 231 for details of SP1 install.

When the install completes, the changes are not highly obvious. One small but visible difference involves the Start menu. Before SP1, it included Search in the list of system folders.

After SP1, the Search command is no longer featured. It is completely removed, not just hidden. However, you can still search using the Search Box just above the Start button.

16

The maintenance level is shown in the computer details which can be viewed using the Welcome Center (see page 23).

1 On the pre-SP1 system, select View Computer Details in Welcome Center and click Show More Details

Hot tip

Another way to check the level of your system is to run the WinVer command. Just click Start, type winver and press Enter.

2 Repeat this for the system after SP1 has been installed

Don't forget

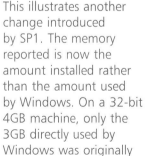

This illustrates another change introduced by SP1. The memory reported is now the amount installed rather than the amount used by Windows. On a 32-bit 4GB machine, only the 3GB directly used by Windows was originally reported. Now you see the full 4GB.

3 Note that the details now specify Service Pack 1 explicitly

Using Your Mouse

The mouse is the usual pointing device used to communicate with your computer, it is an integral part of the user interface.

Right mouse button

Wheel

Left mouse button

LED (Light Emitting Diode)

The typical Windows mouse (like the Microsoft IntelliMouse Optical, shown above) includes the standard two buttons plus a wheel sited between them. Use your index finger to operate the small wheel. This provides an extra level of speed and control when scrolling up and down documents or even web pages - it's much faster than clicking on the scroll arrows displayed. You can even use the wheel to zoom into images and text.

To use a mouse, first place it on a flat surface or a mouse mat. You will notice an arrow-headed pointer (⇖) moving on your screen as you move the mouse.

To make a selection, move the mouse pointer on top of an item and then press and release (or click) the left mouse button. Sometimes you can click twice in rapid succession (double-click) to open a folder, window or a program.

A mouse will usually have at least one more button on the right (called the right mouse button). This provides additional facilities – for example, a click of the second mouse button (right-click) when it is over an appropriate object will display a shortcut menu of related options for further selection.

A mouse can also be used to move items on the screen. This is achieved by first moving the mouse pointer over an item. Then, press and hold down the left mouse button and move the mouse to position the item. Finally, once you see the item in the new location, release the mouse button. This technique is termed dragging.

We will be using the terms click, double-click, right-click and drag throughout this book, to refer to the mouse operations described above.

Starting Windows Vista

When you start up your computer, the Welcome screen will be displayed to request your user sign on details.

1 Click your user name (or the associated picture)

2 If there's a password specified for this user account, type this, then press Enter (or click the arrow)

3 If you mistype the password, click OK and try again. This time a password hint (if defined) will appear

Hot tip

Several users can share the same computer, each with a separate account. See page 184 to create user accounts.

Don't forget

Whenever you start a systems activity, such as adding a new user, you'll be asked for an administrator password or for permission to continue, if you are an administrator.

Beware

If you cannot remember your password, you'll need someone with an administrator account to reset it for you.

Switching Users

If you have a number of user accounts defined on the computer, several accounts can be active at the same time – you don't need to close your programs and log off to be able to switch to another user and it's easy to switch back and forth.

1 Click the Start button, click the down arrow next to the Lock button, and select the Switch User option

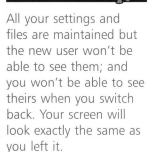

Don't forget

All your settings and files are maintained but the new user won't be able to see them; and you won't be able to see theirs when you switch back. Your screen will look exactly the same as you left it.

2 Another user account may now be selected

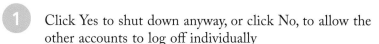

3 Alternatively, for fast user switching, press the Windows logo key + L, to lock the current user, then click the Switch User button on the logon panel and select the other account

Shut down

When you turn off your computer (see page 33), you'll be warned if there are other user accounts still logged on to the computer.

1 Click Yes to shut down anyway, or click No, to allow the other accounts to log off individually

Beware

If the other accounts have data files open, shutting down without logging them off could cause them to lose information.

2 Getting Started

In this chapter, the new look Desktop and Start menu are explained. Then the extensive online help system is covered including how to get outside support if all else fails. Activation is discussed and the new power off options are explored.

The Desktop

If you have a fresh installation (not upgraded from a previous version) your Windows Vista desktop should not have any icons except the Recycle Bin. However, you can display standard icons or add your own shortcut icons for programs that you use frequently – see page 94.

The Welcome Center will be displayed each time you startup (see page 23). There's also a Sidebar on the right for quick access to information and to Gadgets (mini-applications). See page 182.

At the left on the bottom, you'll find the Start button (disguised as a Windows logo). Click the Start button to select your programs and files, change settings, get help and support or logoff and shutdown (see page 33).

The Quick Launch toolbar has tools such as Show Desktop and you can insert shortcuts.

The Taskbar contains a button for each active program or open window, allowing you to Restore, Maximize, Close etc.

Finally, there's the Language bar and the notification area with the system icons.

The Welcome Center

The Welcome Center presents all the common tasks that you need to carry out to complete the configuration of your new PC. It appears automatically at Startup, with 6 tasks displayed.

1   Click the link to Show all items and display the remaining tasks

2   Click a task (e.g. Add new users) to see a more detailed description. The activation link at the right changes appropriately (in this case to Add user accounts)

3   To start a task, click the activation link for the selected task or double-click any task

4   You can stop the Welcome Center from loading if you clear the box at the bottom, labelled "Run at startup"

Don't forget

The Welcome Center is displayed in all of the business and consumer editions of Windows Vista.

Hot tip

You will still be able to open the Welcome Center, from Systems and Maintenance category in the Control Panel.

23

The Start Button

The Start button provides access to all activities if required, but the main display only shows the most frequently used programs and folders. These are the items that you're likely to want to work with and therefore it avoids unnecessary clutter.

On the right you'll see the user account picture and the user name, plus the main folders and functions. Note the change from My Documents, My Pictures (used in previous versions of Windows) to the plain form of Documents, Pictures etc.

Hot tip

At the top of the list are fixed items that are always there, so you can launch them quickly. Internet and email are provided by default and you can add your own shortcuts (see page 95).

Don't forget

The entries in the middle are likely to change, since they show shortcuts to programs you have recently used.

Don't forget

Place your mouse pointer over All Programs to access all your installed programs or begin typing the program name in the Instant Search field (see page 91).

24

Click the Start button (or press the Windows key on its own) to display the Start menu from where you start programs, access files, customize settings, connect to the Internet and much more.

Help and Support Center

1 Click Start and then click the Help and Support button or press the F1 key from the desktop

Hot tip

If you click the Help button in any folder, it will open the Help and Support Center positioned at a relevant topic.

Don't forget

If you'd like to browse the Help system, select the Table of Contents or click Troubleshooting to help you diagnose and fix technical problems.

2 Click a general topic in the Find an answer section, for example Windows Basics

3 You'll see an organized list of topics and sub-topics, for example Desktop fundamentals, with sub-topics such as The desktop (overview)

Hot tip

If Help doesn't have the answer, it can still help you to contact a friend or to contact Microsoft to get more assistance (see page 31).

...cont'd

When you select a sub-topic, an article is displayed with links to sections within the document.

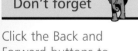

④ Click the link to Working with desktop icons

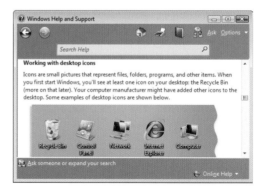

⑤ Some links expand in place, rather than displaying another section

Search Help

If you don't find the topic you're looking for in the topics or contents list, use the search capability within Help and Support.

1 From anywhere in the Help and Support Center, click in the Search box and type a word or phrase

2 Press Enter, or click the Spy Glass button to the right of the box, to search the help information

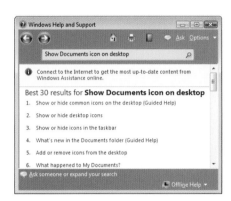

3 The first 30 results will be listed. The better matches will be towards the top of the list. Click one of the entries

Don't forget

If you select Get Online Help (see page 26), you will be able to get the most up to date information.

Hot tip

Note that the color changes for items that you have already reviewed, in the results list and in the See Also lists attached to the individual entries.

Don't forget

Scroll down to the bottom of an entry to find related items listed under the See Also heading.

Guided Help

Windows offers interactive Guided Help for various Windows tasks.

 Click an entry that offers to give you Guided Help

Click the automatic option, to see all the steps displayed

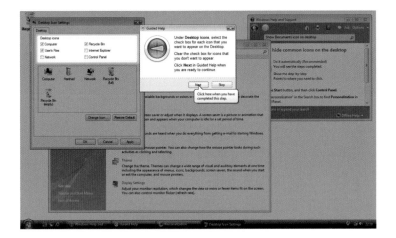

The Guided Help pauses where input is required from you. Click Next when you have completed the entries

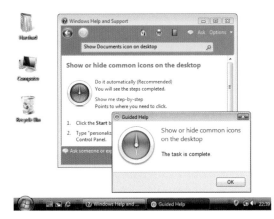

Ask Someone

If you can't solve your problem by using the self-help features discussed in the previous four pages, then you need further assistance. There are several ways you can get this:

1. Open the Help and Support Center (see page 25) or click Home if the Center is already open

Hot tip

There's a quick link to Ask someone or expand your search, at the foot of the screen in any part of the Help and Support Center.

2. Click Windows Remote Assistance to invite someone you trust to help you. You could also offer to help someone

Hot tip

It's likely that your friend or work colleague has encountered the same problems as you've been experiencing. Therefore, with your permission, they can access your system and see your desktop in the hope that they'll be able to help. For Remote Assistance to work, you must both be running Windows Vista.

3. You can send the invitation by email. However, if you use web based email, you should save it as a file

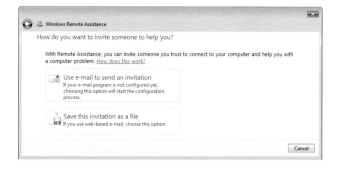

Beware

You must only share control of your system with an individual or company you really trust.

...cont'd

4 You must provide a password, since all communications in Remote Assistance are password controlled and encrypted

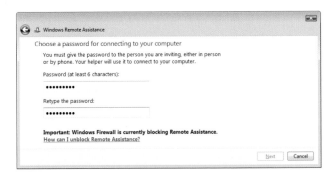

5 Remote Assistance will start up your email software, initiate setup if necessary, then create an invitation

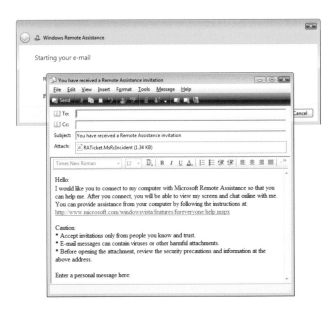

6 Insert the email address, a greeting and a message then click the Send button. Your computer will then wait for an incoming connection

More Support Options

1 Click More Support Options to see other ways in which you can get help, in addition to Remote Assistance

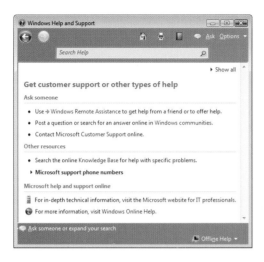

Hot tip

Since Windows Vista is such a recent product, it is likely that the facilities offered will change and develop over time. Go to www.microsoft.com and search for Windows Vista online help, to get the most current details.

- Post questions and view answers at online Windows communities

- Contact Microsoft Customer Support to report problems and request solutions

- Search the online Knowledge Base for specific problems

- Visit the Microsoft website for IT professionals, where you'll find a range of technical resources for Windows Vista

- Explore the Windows Online Help website

Hot tip

You can contact a Microsoft Support Professional via the Internet. You'll be asked to submit all the relevant information to enable Microsoft to understand your problem and provide a solution.

Product Activation

You'll have 14 days to activate Windows Vista after installing it. If you don't activate it within this time then you'll not be able to use Windows until you do activate it. To check the status:

Hot tip

The purpose of Product Activation is to reduce software piracy and to ensure that a licensed copy is used on one PC.

Hot tip

Activation takes under a minute to complete over the Internet and no personal details are collected. If you don't have Internet access you can choose to complete the activation over the phone.

Don't forget

If your copy of Windows Vista was pre-installed by the computer supplier, activation may already have been carried out on your behalf.

1 Select View your computer details in the Welcome Center and scroll down to the bottom

2 If Windows Vista is awaiting activation, click the link, then click Activate Windows online now

3 When activation completes, you'll be told that your copy of Windows Vista has now been validated as genuine

4 When you revisit the Welcome Center, you'll find that the status has been updated accordingly

Turn Off Your Computer

To turn off your computer:

1 Click the Start button, then click the Start menu Power button. Note the split-circle image on the button

Your work is saved, the display turns off and the computer goes into a low power state, sleep mode. This takes just a few seconds. To wake your computer up:

2 Press the hardware power button on your computer systems unit. Your computer starts up in seconds, usually at the Welcome sign on screen and you can resume work

If you'd prefer the Shut down action, with a complete power-off:

3 Select Start, type Power Options in the Start Search box and press Enter, to open Control Panel, Power Options

4 Click Change plan settings (for the active power plan)

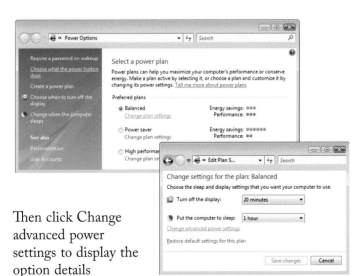

5 Then click Change advanced power settings to display the option details

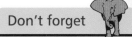

Don't forget

Windows Vista's default power-off state is Sleep mode, which records the contents of memory to the hard disk (just like Hibernate) but also maintains the memory for a period of time (as in XP's Standby mode).

33

Beware

The option "Choose what the power button does" (listed at the left) only applies to the hardware power button, not to the Start menu power button.

...cont'd

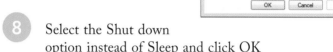

6 Click the plus [+] next to "Power buttons and lid" to expand the list

7 Click the plus [+] next to "Start menu power button" to expand this

8 Select the Shut down option instead of Sleep and click OK

Now when you click Start, the Start menu power button is in Shut down rather than Sleep mode. Note the full-circle image.

Lock your Computer
If you are leaving your desk for a short while, you can lock your keyboard by clicking Start, Lock (or by pressing the Windows key + L). This is only useful if you have a password assigned to your account.

Shut down
If you have the power button set to Sleep, but want, on occasion, to shut down your computer, click the arrow next to the Lock button and then click Shut down.

Restart
With this option, also on the Lock menu, your work is saved and your computer is shut down. However, it immediately starts up again. Select this option after making changes to some of your Windows settings, to put the revisions into effect or after installing certain programs.

The Lock menu also offers the Switch User, Log Off, Lock and Hibernate options.

3 Basic Controls

Most of what you do in Windows Vista will be done using a menu, dialog box or a window. This chapter shows you how you can use these structures, and in particular how you control and manage all the windows used for files, folders and programs.

Menus

Most of the windows will have a Menu bar near the top, displaying the menu options relevant to that particular window. Simply click on a menu option to reveal a drop-down list of further options within it. As an example, we will look at the View menu from the Documents windows.

Beware

The Menu bar is not normally displayed in folder windows, though you can choose to turn it on (see page 38). It is always on for Windows applications, such as WordPad or Paint.

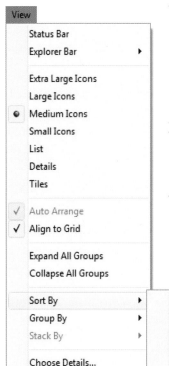

A bullet shows an option to be active but only one option can be selected from a group. Clicking another option from the group will automatically turn off the previously selected one.

A tick shows that an option is active. To deactivate an option with a tick next to it, click on it. Click on it again to activate it.

The forward arrow indicates that there is another linked menu for selection. Move the mouse arrow onto the option to see it.

The ellipse (i.e. ...) indicates that if this option is selected, an associated window with further selections will be displayed.

Hot tip

If an option is dimmed out, it cannot be used at this particular time or is not appropriate.

Hot tip

Other examples of shortcut keys are:
Ctrl+X – Cut
Ctrl+C – Copy
Ctrl+V – Paste
Ctrl+A – Select All
Ctrl+Z – Undo
Ctrl+Y – Redo

Some options may have shortcut keys next to them, so you can use these instead of clicking on the entries with your mouse.

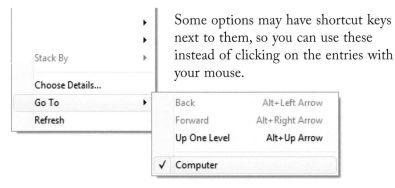

Dialog Boxes

Although simple settings can be made quickly from menu options, other settings need to be made from windows displayed specifically for this purpose. These are called dialog boxes.

Hot tip

These examples are from the Folder Options dialog box. Select Tools, Folder options from the Menu bar, or Organize, Folder and Search Options from the Command bar.

Tabs

Some dialog boxes are divided into two or more tabs (sets of options). Only one tab can be viewed at a time

Check boxes

Click on as many as required. A tick indicates that the option is active. If you click it again it will be turned off. If an option is dimmed, you cannot select it.

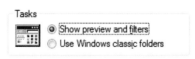

Radio buttons

Only one out of a group of radio buttons can be selected. If you click on another radio button, the previously selected one is automatically turned off.

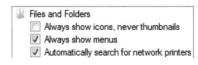

Command buttons

OK will save the settings selected and close the dialog box or window. Cancel will close without saving the amended settings. Apply will save the settings selected so far but will not close, enabling you to make further changes.

Spin boxes

Spin boxes let you type or select numbers only. They usually have arrow buttons to allow you to increment or decrement values.

Hot tip

This spin box is from the Taskbar and Start Menu Properties dialog box (see page 92).

37

Structure of a Window

You can have a window containing icons for further selection or a window that displays a screen from a program. All these windows are similar in their structure, though Windows Vista does add features which do not yet appear in all Windows applications.

Command bar

Navigation pane

Details pane

Forward and Back

Address bar

Search box

Title bar area

Minimize, Maximize/Restore Close

Scroll Up arrow

Slider

Window resize pointers

Scroll bars will only appear when there are items that cannot fit into the current size of the window. Here only a vertical scroll bar is needed.

If you move the mouse pointer over any edge of a window, the pointer changes shape and becomes a double-headed resize pointer – drag it to change the size of a window (see page 42).

Double-click on an icon to open a window relating to it, in this case a WordPad application window. This window has a Menu bar, a toolbar, two scroll bars, a title in the Title bar area and a Control icon at the top left of the title.

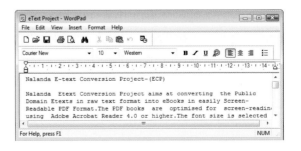

Moving a Window

As long as a window is not maximized, i.e. occupying the whole screen, you can move it. This is especially useful if you have several windows open and need to organize your desktop.

1 Move the mouse pointer over the Title bar of a window

Hot tip

If you have two monitors attached to your system, you can extend your desktop onto the second monitor by dragging a window from one monitor to the other.

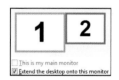

2 Drag the mouse pointer across the desktop (left-click and hold the mouse button down as you move)

3 When the window is in the desired location, release the mouse button

Show window content while dragging

You can see the whole window move, using the option to Show windows contents while dragging. If you switch off that feature, in the Appearance Settings, you'll see just a frame move, until you release the mouse button (as illustrated above).

Restoring a Window

A window can be maximized to fill the whole screen, minimized to a button on the Taskbar or restored to the original size.

Maximized window

Original size window

Maximize button

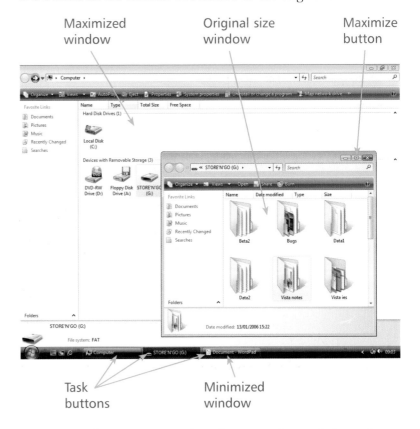

Task buttons

Minimized window

When a window is maximized or the original size, click on the minimize button (left of the top-right three buttons) to reduce the window to a Task button. This will create space on the desktop for you to work in other windows. When you want to restore the reduced window, simply click on its button on the Taskbar.

The middle button (out of the three) is the maximize button or – if the window is already maximized – the button changes to the restore button.

Switching Windows

If you have several windows open on your desktop, one will be active. This will be the foremost window and it has its Title bar, Menu bar and outside window frame highlighted. If you have more than one window displayed on the desktop, click anywhere inside a window that is not active to activate it or switch to it.

Hot tip

The contrast between the active window and the other windows is not very pronounced in the Windows Vista color scheme, but the red Close button helps.

Active task button   Active window

Another method of switching windows is to use the Taskbar at the bottom. Every window that is open has a button created automatically on the Taskbar. Therefore, it does not matter if the window you want to switch to is overlaid with others and you cannot see it. Just click on the button for it in the Taskbar and the window will be moved to the front and made active.

Hot tip

If you have too many windows open so that their task buttons don't fit on the Taskbar, then similar types of task buttons will be grouped together (see page 96).

You can also hold down the Alt key and press tab one or more times. This displays all the windows and selects the next one in turn. Release the Alt key when the window you need is selected. Note that pressing Alt+tab once will act as a toggle, that switches you back and forth between the first two windows in the series.

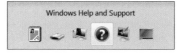

Resizing a Window

If a window is not maximized or minimized, it can be resized.

Hot tip

Resize and move all the windows on your desktop to the way you prefer to work.

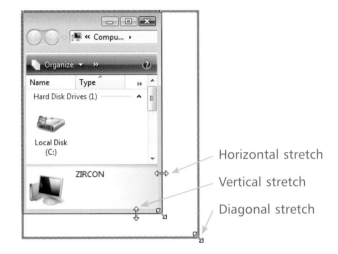

Horizontal stretch

Vertical stretch

Diagonal stretch

Don't forget

Some windows are fixed and cannot be resized. These include dialog boxes and applications, such as the Windows Calculator.

1 Place the mouse arrow anywhere on the edge of a window or on any of the corners. The pointer will change to a double-headed resize pointer

2 Drag the pointer outwards to increase the size of the window or inwards to reduce the size. Release the mouse button when the window is the desired size

Arranging Windows

If you have several windows open on your desktop and you want to automatically rearrange them neatly, rather than resize and move each one individually, use the Cascade or Tile options.

Hot tip

To get rid of the clutter quickly, choose Show the Desktop from the Taskbar shortcut menu.

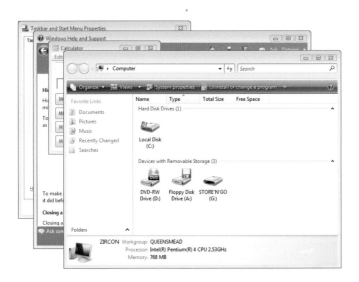

1   Right-click on the Taskbar to display a shortcut menu and select one of the options

Don't forget

Dialog boxes and some applications are not resized, minimized windows are not included.

43

2   Cascade Windows overlaps all open windows, revealing the title bar areas and resizes the windows equally

3   Show Windows Stacked resizes windows equally and displays them across the screen in rows

4   Show Windows Side by Side resizes windows equally and displays them across the screen in columns

Hot tip

If you have a grouped task button (see page 96), right-click on it to Cascade or Tile the windows it contains, minimized windows included.

Arranging Icons

You can rearrange the order of the items in your folders in many different ways.

Don't forget

To make more space in your folder to see all the contents, click Organize, Layout and deselect all the extra information, in this example Details and Navigation panes.

1 Right-click in a clear area (of the desktop or folder window) to display a shortcut menu

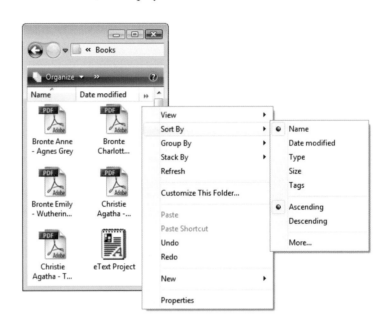

Hot tip

Select View to get all the icon size options. Auto Arrange will reposition icons when you change the window size. Align to Grid will snap icons to an invisible grid and so they will be in alignment with each other.

2 Move the pointer over Sort By, to reveal the submenu of sorting options and click, e.g. the Name option, to sort all the file icons in ascending name order

3 Select Name a second time and the files will be sorted in descending name order

Group By

You can select Group By for folders, but not the Desktop. This groups your files and folders alphabetically by name, size, type, etc. (see page 61 for details). This option is used in the Computer folder, to sort devices by type.

Scrolling

If a window is not big enough to display all the information within it, then a Scroll bar will appear automatically. Use it to see the contents of a window not immediately in view.

Scroll arrow

Scroll slider

Scroll bar

Scroll arrow

45

Don't forget

Depending on the type of content, you may have a horizontal scroll bar, with or instead of the vertical scroll bar illustrated.

The size of the Scroll box (or Slider) in relation to the Scroll bar indicates how much of the total contents are in view. The position tells you which portion is in view.

1   Drag the Scroll box along the Scroll bar towards one of the two Scroll arrows to scroll in that direction

      or

Hot tip

If your mouse has a scroll wheel, you can use this to scroll. Towards you is downwards, away from you is upwards.

2   Click on the Scroll bar to display the next window's amount of information towards the nearest Scroll arrow

      or

3   Click on one of the Scroll arrows to scroll just a little in that direction. Hold down your mouse button to scroll continuously

Closing a Window

When you've finished with a window you will need to close it. There are several ways of doing this – use the method that's easiest and the most appropriate at the time.

For an Open window
If the top right corner of the window is visible on the desktop:

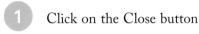 Click on the Close button

For a Minimized window
For a window that's hidden behind other windows:

1 Right click on the associated task button

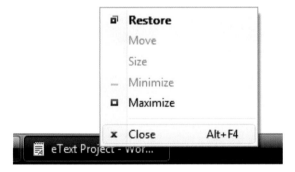

2 Click on Close from the shortcut menu

From the Control icon
This applies to program windows.

1 Click on the Control icon (top left corner)

2 Click on Close from the shortcut menu

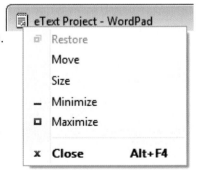

From the keyboard
You can close any type of window with this key combination.

1 Press Alt+F4 to close the active window

4 Windows Explorer

You'll find yourself using Windows Explorer to browse all the information on your computer and on the local network, whether you start from Computer or Documents or any other folder, or open Windows Explorer explicitly as an application. In all cases, you can modify the view, sort the contents and customize the style and appearance.

Windows Explorer

It may not be obvious, but Windows Explorer is the first program you use, when you run Windows Vista. It is the application that displays the Welcome Center (see page 23). It also manages the folders listed on the Start menu (see page 88), among other tasks.

To illustrate the range of functions that it supports:

1 Open programs (e.g. Calculator, NotePad, Paint, WordPad) or folders (e.g. Computer, Documents, Music, Pictures) from the Start menu

2 Windows of the same type will be grouped. You'll find there are several identified as Windows Explorer

3 Click the down arrow to show the names of these windows

This makes Windows Explorer the way to investigate the contents of your computer (and your network), whichever location you decide to start from. Because the Explorers all use the same program, the techniques you learn when you open Computer, for example, will apply also in Documents or Pictures, and when you open Windows Explorer from All Programs, Accessories (see page 88) or by using the shortcut key (Windows key + E).

Hot tip

Windows Explorer (also known as Explorer) is the program Explorer.exe. You may also see specialised folders such as Documents, Music and Games, referred to as Explorers.

Hot tip

This example also includes the Welcome Center, Control Panel and Personalization (to get this right-click the desktop and select Personalize).

Don't forget

Windows Explorer is also responsible for search functions, displaying the desktop icons and wallpaper, Start menu, Taskbar and Control Panel (features that are known collectively as the Windows Shell).

Computer Folder

The best way to look for any of your files, regardless of where they are stored, involves using the Computer folder. To open this:

1 Double-click the Computer icon on the desktop (if it is displayed)

or

Click the Start button and select Computer from the Start menu

Navigation pane   Location   Search box

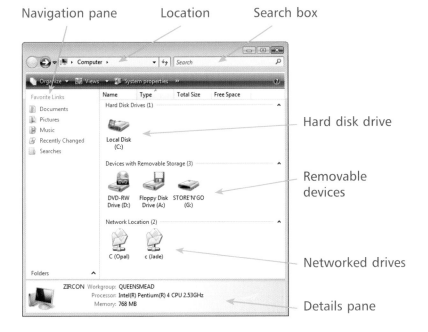

Hard disk drive

Removable devices

Networked drives

Details pane

2 Select the hard disk drive icon to see the total and free space available, displayed in the Details pane

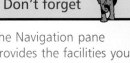

3 The contents of the Command bar also change, to suit the type of device you select, e.g. the DVD-RW device

49

Don't forget

In previous versions of Windows, this folder was known as My Computer. It also featured shared folders, but these are not displayed under Vista.

Don't forget

The Navigation pane provides the facilities you need to move between folders. It contains the Favorites list and/or the Folder list, depending on the layout in use.

Hot tip

The Command bar adds the Eject button for a DVD or CD drive, plus the Burn to Disc button for rewriter capability.

Exploring Drives

Explore the contents of any drive from the Computer Folder.

Don't forget

As you explore a drive, the contents of the Command bar change to suit the particular entry selected.

1 Select one of the drive icons, for example, the USB storage device

Hot tip

For some of the illustrations, the Details pane has been turned off (see page 49). This gives extra space for the contents.

2 Double-click the USB device icon (or select and press Enter) to display the files and folders that it contains

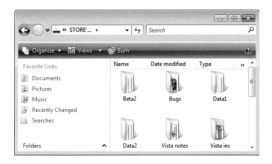

Don't forget

Press the Back arrow to return to the previous folder. See page 56 for more ways to navigate using the Address bar.

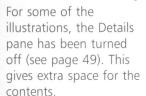

3 Double-click a folder entry (e.g. Data2) and select one of the files that it contains (e.g. the Overview document)

Folders List

You can see all the folder entries in Computer in a structured list.

1 Click the Folders button at the bottom of the Navigation pane

2 The folder list, from the desktop and with all the drives, will be displayed, with the current drive or folder selected

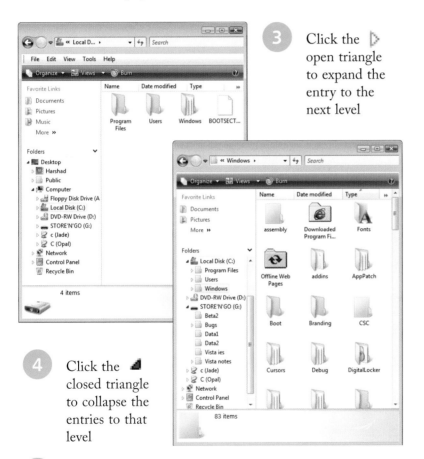

3 Click the ▷ open triangle to expand the entry to the next level

4 Click the ◢ closed triangle to collapse the entries to that level

5 From the folder list, you can explore different devices, the Users folder, the Public folder, Network drives etc.

6 Click the Folders button, at the top of the folders list to close the list back down again

Don't forget

In previous versions of Windows Explorer, this was known as the folder tree.

51

Hot tip

Resize the navigation pane and folder list, using stretch arrows as you do to resize other windows (see page 42).

Opening Windows Explorer

The Computer folder is just one way of opening Windows Explorer. There are a number of other ways.

1 Select another folder from the Start menu, such as Documents, Pictures or Music, and Windows Explorer will open with your copy of that folder

2 Right-click the Computer icon on the desktop and select Explore. The Computer folder opens with the Folders list

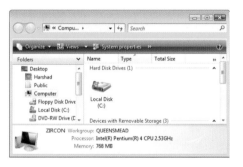

3 Press the Windows key + E combination, and the Computer folder opens with the Folders list

4 Select Start, All Programs, Accessories, Windows Explorer. The Documents folder will open

5 Right-click the Start button and select Explore. The Start menu folder for the current user opens

Favorite Links

When the Folders list is closed, the Navigation pane displays Favorite Links and saved Searches. The default links are to the Documents, Pictures and Music folders, but you can add links.

1 Locate the folder which you want to add to the Favorite Links and drag it onto the list

2 Select and drag entries in the list, to rearrange them into a different order

3 Right-click a Favorite Link and select Rename, if you need to provide a more descriptive title for the entry

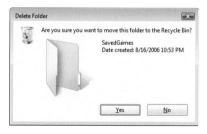

4 Right-click an item and click Delete (or select the item and press the Delete key) to remove an entry from the Favorite Links list

5 To remove all added links and return to the original settings, right-click in the space below the list and select Restore Default Favorite Links

Open Favorite Links Folder
Restore Default Favorite Links

6 Select Open Favorite Links Folder, to view or edit the shortcut files in their folder

Hot tip

The Navigation pane also contains saved searches (see page 54).

Hot tip

Make sure that the black marker bar is positioned where you want the new link to appear.

Don't forget

Changing the name in the Favorites list does not affect the actual folder name.

Saved Searches

At the end of the Favorite Links you'll see two entries:

● Recently Changed – a list of documents and files that you've been working with

● Searches – a list of standard searches that have been saved for your use (one of which is the Recently Changed entry)

 To open a saved search, click Searches in the Navigation pane and then double-click the search you want to carry out, for example, Recent Documents

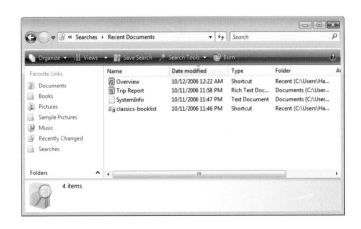

The search is carried out as defined and the results are displayed in the Searches folder

To create and save your own search:

1. Open the place you want to search (e.g. the hard disk drive in Computer) and type your search value (e.g. *.jpg)

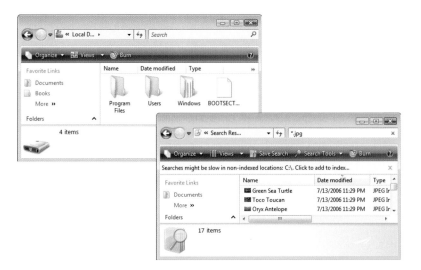

Hot tip

For more information on the options available when searching for files and folders see page 84.

2. Matches are displayed as you type. When you see the results you want, click Save Search on the toolbar

Don't forget

You can Index the files on your hard disk drive, to speed up searches.

3. In the File Name box, type a name for the search, then click Save. Your search now appears in the Searches list

4. If you'll be using this search frequently drag it onto the Favorite Links, so it is immediately to hand

55

Address Bar

The Address bar at the top of each folder displays the current folder address, as a set of names separated by arrows, and offers another way to navigate between folders.

Don't forget

Press the Back arrow to select the previous folder or click the down arrow to select from the list of folders viewed.

1 To go to a location that's named in the address, click on that name in the address bar, e.g. Users

2 To select a subfolder of a folder named in the Address bar, click the arrow to the right of that folder

Hot tip

If the current folder appears in the list, its name will be highlighted in bold print.

3 Click one of the subfolders to open it instead of the current folder

New Location

1 Click in the Address bar, in the space to the right of the set of names and the full folder path is displayed

Don't forget

You can switch to exploring the Internet, by typing a web page address. Internet Explorer will be launched in a separate window (see page 113).

2 Type the complete folder path, e.g. C:\Users\Public and then press Enter

If you want a common location such as Computer, you can just type the name alone. The list of common names includes:

Computer	Contacts	Control Panel
Documents	Favorites	Games
Music	Pictures	Recycle Bin

Customize Layout

We've seen different views of the Navigation pane and the Details pane for Windows Explorer, but these aren't the only panes available. There's also a Search pane and a Preview pane, to enable you to find and select specific files quickly and easily.

To select which panes are displayed:

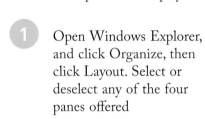

1 Open Windows Explorer, and click Organize, then click Layout. Select or deselect any of the four panes offered

Don't forget

This menu also offers the Menu Bar option, to display the old-style Menu bar permanently. Pressing the Alt key also displays the Menu bar, but temporarily, just for one use.

Navigation pane   Menu bar   Search pane   Folder contents

Hot tip

The Games folder is an exception to the normal rule, since it does not feature the Navigation pane in its layout.

Details pane   Preview pane

2 Click any entry in the folder contents, to see an image of it in the Preview pane

3 Drag the separator lines between the panes, using the stretch arrows (see page 51) to resize the panes

Folder Contents

The entries in any of the folders you look at with Windows Explorer will be other folders and/or files (documents, pictures, programs etc.). The way these are presented will differ from folder to folder, usually based on the type of files normally contained:

Document and program files

Hot tip

In these examples, the Navigation and Details panes have been turned off (see page 38) to allow us to concentrate on the folder contents.

Medium icons

Image and picture files

Don't forget

The display style for the contents in your own versions of these folders may be different but, whatever the settings, you can make changes to suit your preferences (see page 64).

Large icons

Audio and music files

Details – artist, genre, album etc.

Hot tip

Although both these folders use Details view, they show different sets of attributes appropriate to the type of file. Note that the other folder views also quote attribute headings to suit their file types.

Search results

Details – author, type, etc.

Changing Views

You can change the size and appearance of the file and folder icons in your folders, using the Views menu on the Command bar.

1 Open the folder you would like to change and click the arrow next to Views on the toolbar

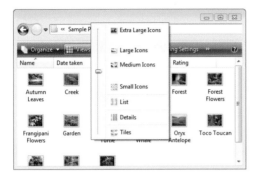

Hot tip

Click the Views button on the toolbar (not the down arrow), and you will switch to the next view in the sequence: List; Details; Tiles; Large.

2 Click and drag the slider to change the appearance of icons. Changes are applied as the slider moves

Hot tip

You can select intermediate positions, but as the slider approaches each of the four icon sizes, it snaps to that position. There are no intermediate positions associated with List, Details or Tiles.

3 Pause at any position, holding the mouse button, to see the effect. Release the mouse button to apply that view

Sorting

Windows allows you to sort your files in any drive or folder by various attributes or descriptors.

 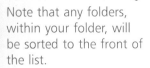
1 Open the folder and click the attribute header that you want to sort by, e.g. Type

2 The entries are sorted into ascending order by the selected attribute. The header is shaded and a down angle added

3 Click the header again, the order is reversed and the header now shows an up angle (direction of sort)

4 The contents will remain sorted in the selected sequence, even if you select a different folder to view

Grouping

1 If you have a sorted folder, select the header for the sort attribute (see page 60) and click the down arrow

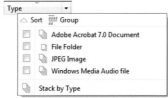

(see page 60)

2 Click the Group button, the sorted contents will be grouped in the ranges specified

3 To group by another attribute, right-click the folder area, click Group By and select another descriptor or click More and add additional attributes

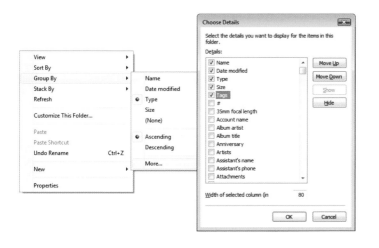

4 Change the order the attributes are displayed by selecting them and using the Move Up and Move Down buttons

Folder Options

You can change the appearance and the behavior of your folders by adjusting the folder settings.

1 From any folder, click Organize and select Folder and Search Options

2 Click Use Windows classic folders to turn off the Details pane and display the Menu bar for all folders

3 Choose Open each folder in its own window, to keep multiple folders open at the same time

4 If you want items to open as they do on a web page, select Single-click to open an item (point to select)

5 Click Apply to try out the change without closing Folder Options. Select Restore Defaults then Apply, to reset all these options to their default values

There are further settings that can be applied to the current folder (from which the Folder Options were opened).

1 From the Folder Options dialog box, click the View tab

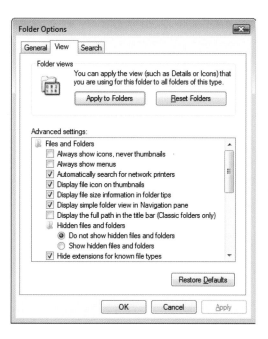

2 Clear the option Display file icon on thumbnails, then click Apply to remove the branding that indicates the file type on the file previews

3 Click Always show icons, never thumbnail previews, press Apply and you may find that you get better performance with the static file icons

4 Click Restore Defaults if you want to undo all changes

Hot tip

Click the Apply to Folders button to apply the current folder view to all folders of the same type. If you open Folder Options from the Control Panel, rather than a folder, this button becomes inactive.

Hot tip

This dialog box provides another place where you can switch on the classic menu bar for folders.

Hot tip

To avoid having to create an individual miniature of each document or image, the standard icon for the file type is displayed.

63

Customizing Folders

1 Open the folder, right-click a clear space within it and select Customize This Folder

  Customize This Folder...

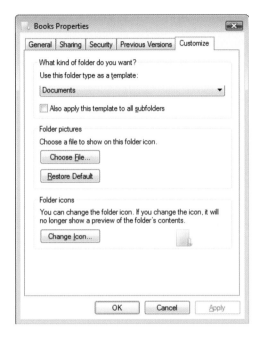

2 Click the down arrow next to Use this folder type as a template, then choose the most relevant type

All Items
Documents
Pictures and Videos
Music Details
Music Icons

3 Click Choose File, locate an image file and click Open and Apply to the folder

Choose File...

5 Manage Files and Folders

Folders can contain other folders as well as files, and Windows treats them in very much the same way. Hence operations such as moving, copying , deleting and searching apply to files and to folders in a similar way, while compressed files (which contain files and folders) are treated as folders in their own right.

Select Files and Folders

To select a single file or folder you simply click on it to highlight it, then you can move, copy or delete it as required (see page 68).

To perform the operation on several files or folders, it is more efficient to select and process a group, rather than one by one.

Sequential files

1 Click to select the first item, press and hold Shift, then click the last item in the range, to highlight the range

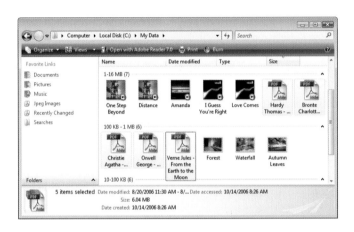

Adjacent Block

1 Drag out a box to cover files you want selected. All the files in that rectangular area will be highlighted

Non-adjacent files

Hot tip

To deselect one file, click it while the Ctrl key is being held down.
To deselect all the files, click once anywhere in the folder outside the selection area.

1 To select several non-adjacent files, click one item, press and hold Ctrl, then click the subsequent items. As you select files, they are highlighted

Partial Sequence

You can combine these techniques to select part of a range.

Beware

If you select a folder, you will also be selecting any files and folders that it may contain.

1 Select a group of sequential files or an adjacent block of files (as described on page 64)

2 Hold down Ctrl, and click to deselect any files in the range that you do not want and to select any extra ones

All Files and Folders

To select all the files (and folders) in the current folder, click Organize and choose Select All or press Ctrl+A.

Copy or Move Files or Folders

You may wish to copy or move some files and folders, to another folder on the same drive, or to another drive. There are several ways to achieve this.

Drag, using the right mouse button

1 Open Windows Explorer, click the Folders button and in the Folders list select the folder containing the files etc.

2 In the folder contents, select the files and folders that you want to copy or move (see page 66)

3 Right-click any one of the selection, drag the files onto the destination folder or drive in the Folders list, so it is highlighted and named, then release to display the menu

4 Click the Move Here or Copy Here option as desired

Drag, using the left mouse button

1 Select the files and folders to be moved or copied

2 Use the left mouse button to drag the selection to the destination drive or folder in the Folders list, in this example the USB storage device

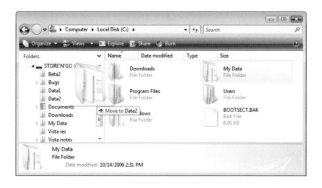

69

3 Press Shift to Move instead of Copy to another drive. Press Ctrl to Copy instead of Move to a folder on the same drive as the source folder

In Summary

Drives	Drag	Drag+Shift	Drag+Ctrl
Same	Move	Move	Copy
Different	Copy	Move	Copy

...cont'd

Using Cut, Copy, Paste

1 Choose the files and folders you want to copy and right-click within the selection

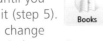
Books

2 From the shortcut menu click Copy or click Cut to move the selection

3 Right-click and click Open for a separate window for the folder in which you want to put the selection

4 Right-click a blank area of the destination folder

5 Click Paste from the menu to complete the copy or move operation

Books - Shortcut

Paste
Paste Shortcut

Keyboard Shortcuts

Cut, Copy and Paste options are also available as keyboard shortcuts. You select files and folders as above, but use these keys in place of the menu selections for Copy, Cut and Paste.

Press this key	To do this
CTRL+C	Copy the selected item
CTRL+X	Cut the selected item
CTRL+V	Paste the selected item
CTRL+Z	Undo an action

Burn to Disc

If your computer has a CD or DVD recorder, you can copy files to a writable disc. This is usually termed burning.

1 Insert a writable CD or DVD disc into the recorder drive

2 When the Autoplay prompt appears, choose Burn files to disc using Windows

3 Click to Show formatting options

4 By default, Windows uses the File System (UDF) format, but for compatibility with other devices, you should choose the Mastered (ISO) format

5 You can now copy or move files to the drive folder. When you have finished adding files, click Burn to disc

Don't forget

The Windows media tools (see pages 196-202) include options to burn images and videos to CD or DVD.

Hot tip

Choose the File System (UDF) format if you plan to leave the disc in the drive, and copy files to it as, for example, an on-going backup.

71

Don't forget

You can use any of the methods described for copying or moving one, or more, files and folders (see page 68).

File Conflicts

When you copy or move files from one folder to another, conflicts may arise. There may already be a file with the same name in the destination folder. To illustrate what may happen:

 Open the Documents folder and the Backups folder

2 Press Ctrl+A in Documents, and Drag the selection onto the Backups folder, to initiate a copy of all the files

3 Windows observes a conflict – this file already exists, with identical size and date information. Select Don't Copy

4 The next case is where the source file is newer and larger than the existing file. Assuming that this is an updated version, click Copy and Replace

Hot tip

Size is not always a good indicator. Document files, for example, may have changes consolidated when resaved, so may appear smaller even though no content has been removed.

5 Here, the file is newer but smaller. Assuming that this is a different Memo, you'd click Copy, but keep both files. The copy is renamed as Memo (2)

6 The Backups folder now has updated copies of all the files, plus an additional file – the second memo

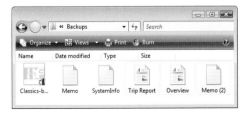

Delete Files and Folders

When you want to remove files or folders, you use the same delete procedures – whatever drive or device the items are stored on.

 1 Select one or more files and folders, selected as described previously (see page 66)

 2 Right-click the selection and click Delete

74

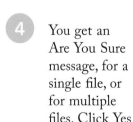

3 Alternatively, having selected the items, click Organize and then select Delete

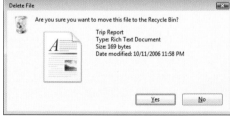

4 You get an Are You Sure message, for a single file, or for multiple files. Click Yes to confirm

If you immediately realize that you have made a mistake deleting one or more files, right-click the folder area and select Undo Delete or press Ctrl+Z, to reverse the last operation. For hard disk items, use the Recycle Bin to retrieve them (see pages 75-77).

The Recycle Bin

The Recycle Bin is, in effect, a folder on your hard disk drive that holds deleted files and folders. They are not physically removed from your hard disk (unless you empty the Recycle Bin or delete specific items from within the Recycle Bin itself). They will remain there, until the Recycle Bin fills up, at which time the oldest deleted files may be finally removed.

The Recycle Bin, therefore, provides a safety net for files and folders you may delete by mistake and allows you to easily retrieve them, even at a later date.

Restoring files

Recycle Bin

① Double-click on the Recycle Bin icon from the desktop or in the Computer folder

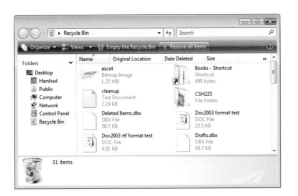

② Click the Restore all items button or select a file and the button changes to Restore this item

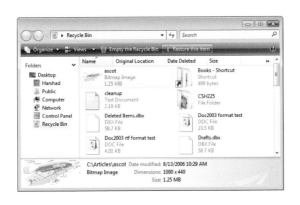

Hot tip

Files and folders that you delete from the Command Prompt, don't go into the Recycle Bin. Also, there's no recycle bin for drives with removable media.

Hot tip

A restored folder will include all the files and subfolders that it held when it was originally deleted.

Don't forget

If you select multiple files or folders (see page 66) the button becomes Restore the selected items.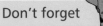

...cont'd

Permanently Erase files

You may want to explicitly delete particular files, perhaps for reasons of privacy and confidentiality.

 Open the Recycle Bin (see page 75)

Select the relevant files and folders, click Organize and then click Delete

Click Yes, to confirm that you want these files permanently deleted (completely removed from the hard disk drive)

Empty the Recycle Bin

If desired, you can remove all of the contents of the Recycle Bin from the hard disk drive.

With the Recycle Bin open, click the Empty the Recycle Bin button

The Recycle Bin icon changes from full to empty, to illustrate the change.

Recycle Bin   Recycle Bin

Bypass the Recycle Bin

If you want to prevent particular deleted files from being stored in the Recycle Bin:

1. Select the files and folders, right-click the selection (as described on page 74) but this time, hold down the Shift key as you select Delete

2. Confirm that you want to permanently delete the selected item or items. "Permanent" means that no copy will be kept

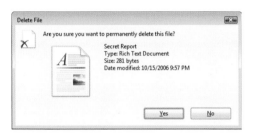

Beware

Take extra care when selecting files and folders, if you are bypassing the Recycle Bin, since you'll have no recovery options.

Deactivate the Recycle Bin

You can tell Windows to always bypass the Recycle Bin.

1. Right-click on the Recycle Bin icon, then click Properties

2. Click the button labelled "Do not move files to the Recycle Bin. Remove files immediately when deleted."

Don't forget

This dialog box also allows you to adjust the amount of disk space allocated to the Recycle Bin, and to suppress the warning message issued when you delete items.

Create a File or Folder

You can create a new folder in a drive, folder or on the desktop.

 1 Select Organize, New Folder. A folder with the name New Folder is added. Overtype this name with your preferred name and press Enter

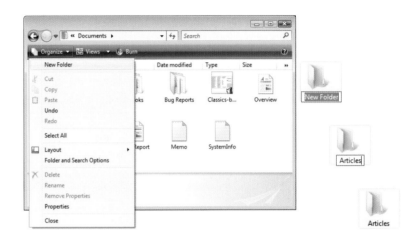

78

To create a new file in a standard format for use with one of the programs installed on your computer.

1 Right-click an empty part of the folder, select New, then choose the specific file type, e.g. Rich Text Document

2 Overtype the file name provided and press Enter

Rename a File or Folder

You can rename a file or folder at any time, by simply editing the current name.

1 Right-click the file/folder, then click Rename, or select the icon and click on the icon name

Hot tip

Use the same method to rename icons on the desktop. You can even rename the Recycle Bin.

2 Either way, the current name will be highlighted. Type a name to delete and replace the current name:

or press the arrow keys to position the typing cursor and edit the existing name:

Don't forget

You must always provide a non-blank file name.

79

3 Press Enter or click elsewhere to confirm the new name

Preserving File Types

When you have file extensions revealed (see page 78) and you create or rename a file or folder, only the name itself and not the file type, will be highlighted. This is to avoid accidentally changing the type of file.

Beware

You can change the file type, but you will be warned that this may make the file unusable.

Backtrack File Operations

If you accidentally delete, rename, copy or move the wrong file or folder, you can undo (reverse) the last operation and preceding operations, to get back to where you started. For example:

Hot tip

Undo mistakes as soon as possible since you'd have to undo subsequent operations first. Also, only a limited amount of undo history is maintained.

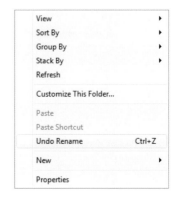

1 Right-click the folder area and select the Undo Rename command that is displayed

Don't forget

The Undo command that is offered, changes depending on which operation was being performed at the time.

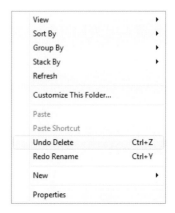

2 Right-click again, this time there's an Undo Delete command to select

Don't forget

If you go back too far, right-click the folder and select the available Redo operation, e.g. Redo Rename.

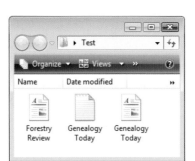

3 The last two operations have now been reversed, putting the files back as they were before

80

File Properties

Every file (and every folder) has information that can be displayed in the Properties dialog box. To display this:

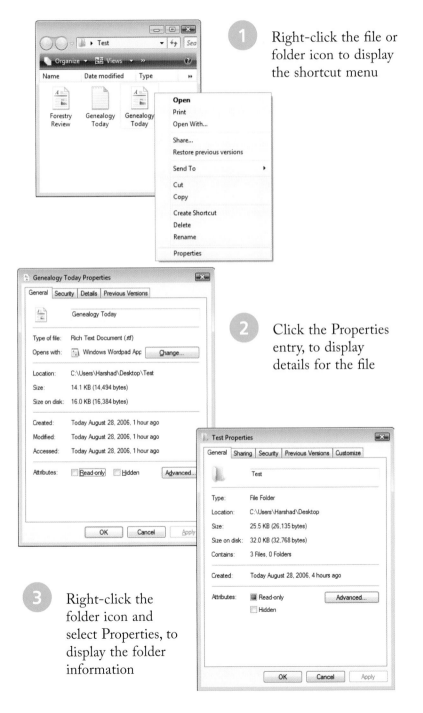

1 Right-click the file or folder icon to display the shortcut menu

2 Click the Properties entry, to display details for the file

3 Right-click the folder icon and select Properties, to display the folder information

Hot tip

The purpose of the Properties dialog box is:
• to display details
• to change settings
for the selected file or folder.

Hot tip

You may find additional entries on your menu, inserted when you install additional programs (see page 99).

Don't forget

Click Security and other tabs, to display more information about the file, and click the Advanced button for additional attributes.

Open Files

You can open a file, using an associated program but without having first to explicitly start that program. There are several ways to do this:

Default Program

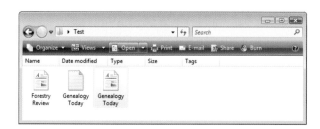

1   Double-click the file icon

2   Right-click the file and click Open from the menu

3   Select the file, then click Open on the Command bar

Alternative Program

You may have several programs that can open a particular file type. To use a different program than the default to open the file:

1   Right-click the file icon and select Open With. Pick a program from the list or click Choose Default Program to set a new default program

2   The same choices are also presented, when you click the down arrow next to the Open button on the Command bar

Recent Items

Quite often you'll want to open a document you have been working on recently. Windows stores details of the latest documents (up to the last 15) you've been using. To find them:

1 Click Start, Recent Items

Hot tip

You can also click the Documents, Pictures or Music for quick access to the items that you have stored in those folders.

2 Click the required document or image from this list

Clear Recent Items

You can clear the history that appears in Recent Items.

1 Right-click the Start button and select Properties

2 Clear the box Store and display a list of recently opened files

Don't forget

To resume recording the list of recent items, re-select the box and click Apply again.

3 Click the Apply button and the list will be cleared. Click OK to exit

Search for Files and Folders

If you are not quite sure where exactly you stored a file, or what the full name is, the folder Search box may be the answer.

1 Open a folder, e.g. Documents, click in the Search box and start typing a word from the file, e.g. invoice

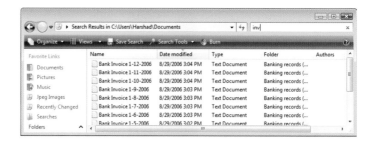

2 If that produces too many files, start typing another word that might appear in the name, e.g. article

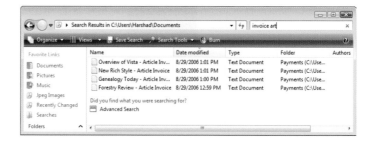

3 If the file is still not found, click Advanced Search and specify broader criteria (e.g. C:\) then click Search

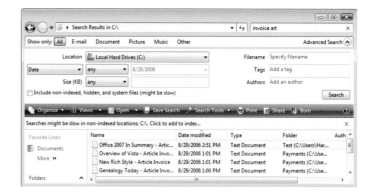

Compressed Folders

This feature allows you to save disk space by compressing files and folders while allowing them to be treated as normal by Windows.

Create a compressed folder:

1 From any folder window click on File, New, Compressed (zipped) Folder

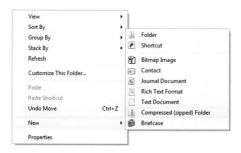

2 A compressed folder is created, with the default name of New Compressed (zipped) Folder.zip

3 Rename it, (see page 79). You can also open, move, or delete it just like any folder

Add files or folders to a compressed folder

 **1** Drag files or folders onto a compressed folder and they will automatically be compressed there

Extract files and folders

1 Open the compressed folder, drag files and folders onto a normal folder and they'll be decompressed. The compressed version still remains in the compressed folder, unless you hold the Shift key as you drag (i.e. Move)

(see page 79)

Hot tip

Compressed folders are distinguished from other folders by a zipper on the folder icon. They are compatible with other zip archive programs, such as Winzip.

Financial records

Don't forget

To create a compressed folder and copy a file into it at the same time: right-click a file, select Send To, Compressed (zipped) Folder. The new compressed folder has the same file name, but a file extension of .zip.

85

Hot tip

The compressed folder is treated like a separate device. By default, files will be copied when they are dragged to, or from, the folder.

...cont'd

Extract All

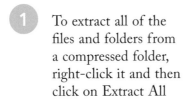

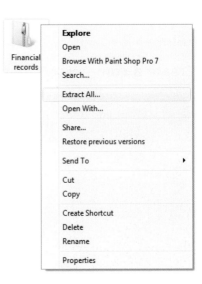

1 To extract all of the files and folders from a compressed folder, right-click it and then click on Extract All

2 Accept or edit the target folder and click Extract. The files and folders are decompressed and transferred

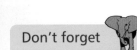
86

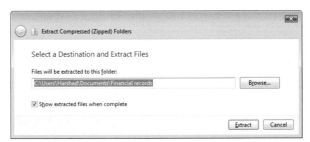

Compressed Item Properties

1 Right-click any file, or folder, in the compressed folder and choose Properties to see the actual versus the compressed size

6 Working with Programs

Windows provides the
operational environment
in which you can run
application programs. It
offers Start menu and search
facilities to help you locate
and run the applications,
and helps you to install,
organize and manage your
programs effectively. It
includes functions such as
the Compatibility Wizard
and Task Manager.

Start and Close Programs

The Windows Logo Start button enables you to quickly start any program installed in your computer.

1 Click on the Start button and the Start menu appears, with the frequently used programs and the Folders list

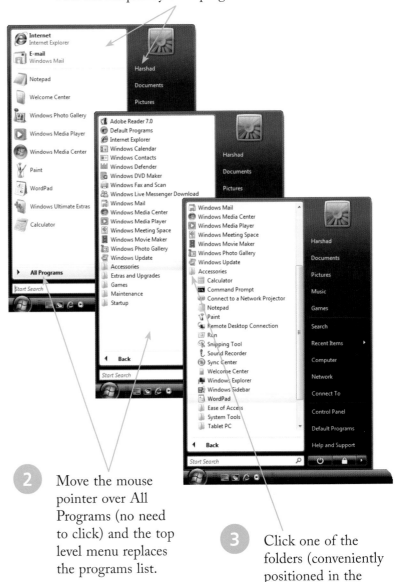

2 Move the mouse pointer over All Programs (no need to click) and the top level menu replaces the programs list.

3 Click one of the folders (conveniently positioned in the lower part of the menu) and it expands to show its contents

4 When you've located the application, click its entry to open the program

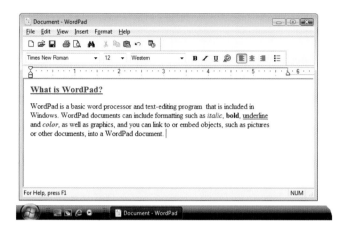

Hot tip

See page 96 for information on the Windows Taskbar grouping feature.

5 A button for the selected program appears on the Taskbar and the program starts in its own window

Close the program

There are several ways to close the program.

1 Click the Close button on the top right of the window

Don't forget

These are analogous to the methods for closing a window (see page 46).

2 Select File, Exit from the Menu

3 Press Alt+F4

4 Click the Control icon, right-click the title bar or right-click the task button and select Close

If the program involved is making changes to a file (e.g. a document in WordPad), you may receive a warning message advising you to Save changes.

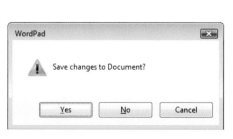

Classic Start Menu

Windows still supports the classic Start menu, where the shortcut folders expand to the right, leaving the previous levels visible, giving you another way to spot the program you want.

To switch to the Classic Start menu view:

1 Right click the Start button and select Properties

2 Click the button labeled Classic Start menu, then click Apply and OK

3 To restore the standard Start menu, open the Taskbar and Start Menu Properties as above, select the button Start Menu and then click OK

Start Searches

The Start menu gives you a very easy way to locate programs (and data files).

1 Click the Start button to open the Start menu

2 Start typing a word that is associated with the program you want, for example View... (no need to click the box)

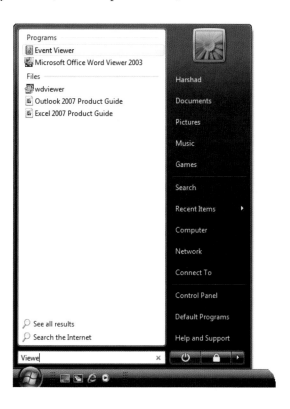

Don't forget

Case does not matter, but it is important to get the spelling right.

Hot tip

Search looks at the program titles in the Start menu and, at file names and contents in the current user name, and in standard folders such as Program Files. You can extend the search scope by specifying the drive letter for an attached device.

3 As you type, relevant programs and data files are displayed. When the one you are seeking appears, click it to start the program (or open the data file using its associated program)

Start Program using Run

With the Run command, you can start any program. This is very handy if you have enabled the classic Start menu (see page 90), which has no Start Search facility. However, it is not normally displayed on the standard Start menu. To add it:

1 Right-click the Start button and select Properties, then click the Customize button

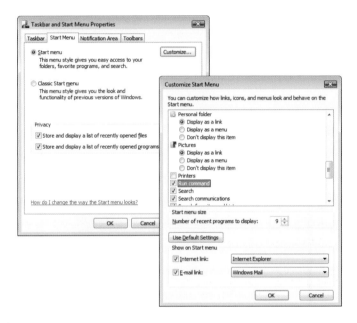

2 Scroll down the list and locate the entry for Run. Click in the box to enable this, then click OK

Using the Run Command

1 Click Start, Run from the standard Start menu or from the classic Start menu

2 Click the down arrow to view previous commands, and pick one of these (if appropriate) instead of typing in a name

3 Select Browse and navigate to the program. It will insert the full path and name into the Open box

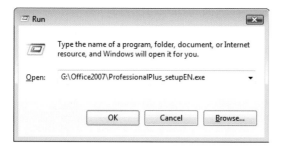

4 Type in the full name of the program, including drive and path, if necessary

5 Click OK to start the program

The program will execute and, in the case of the Setup type of program, may install application programs and add entries to the Start menu. For example, with Microsoft Office 2007, you find:

Create a Shortcut

A Shortcut can provide easy access to a program you use frequently. To place the shortcut on the desktop:

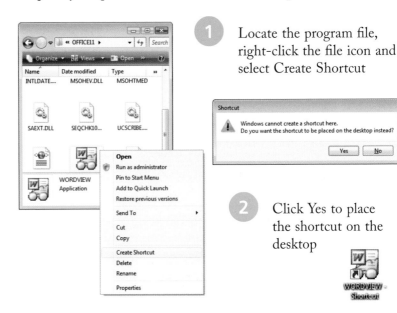

Don't forget

The shortcut copies the original icon, with the addition of a small arrow and the term – Shortcut.

1 Locate the program file, right-click the file icon and select Create Shortcut

2 Click Yes to place the shortcut on the desktop

Shortcuts can also be created to access other objects, including documents, folders, disk drives, printers and network devices.

1 Locate the item and drag its icon onto the desktop (or onto a folder) using the right mouse button

Beware

Windows will not let you create shortcuts in special folders such as Computer, Network or Control Panel.

94

Hot tip

If you delete a shortcut, the file that it relates to is not automatically deleted. The converse is also true – deleting the original item does not remove the shortcut.

2 Drop the icon to display the menu, then select Create Shortcuts Here

STORE'N'GO
(G) - Shortcut

Pin to Start Menu

Another way to get easy access to a program that you use often, is to add it to the top level on the Start menu

1 Right-click a program icon or a shortcut to a program

2 Select Pin to Start Menu

3 For a folder, or folder shortcut, drag the icon onto the Start button. When the Start menu expands, drop the icon at the top – the black line shows the position

Remove Entries

To remove an entry from the Start menu:

1 Right-click the entry and select Unpin from Start Menu

2 For a folder entry, right-click and select Remove from this list

Hot tip

Right-click entries from All Programs or one of its folders, then select Pin to Start Menu. The original entry will remain in place.

Beware

Folders and folder shortcuts do not offer the Pin to Start Menu option.

Don't forget

You can change the name of an entry (right-click and select Rename), and you can drag them to rearrange the sequence.

Taskbar Grouping

Windows creates a task button on the Taskbar for every document you open with a program. Due to the multitasking capabilities of Windows, you can have several programs open at the same time, each with several open documents. This can result in a very cluttered Taskbar, making it difficult to locate a particular task when you need to switch to it.

Taskbar grouping combines all the information for the same program into just one task button. It does this automatically once the number of task buttons builds up to a number that will not comfortably fit on the Taskbar.

Hot tip

To ensure Taskbar Grouping is active, right-click the Taskbar, click Properties and select the box for Group similar taskbar buttons.

Grouped task button

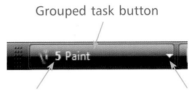

Number of documents grouped into this task button

Click the Group task button to list and select documents

The pop-up menu displays the document name, with an icon to show the program that created it. Click any document to switch to it and bring its window to the forefront.

Right-click the task button to cascade the windows, show them stacked or show them side by side (see page 43). You can also Minimize or Close all document windows, rather than each one individually.

Startup Folder

The Startup feature allows a program or several programs to start automatically when you log on to Windows. Therefore, you can start work straightaway on a program that you always use.

1 Create shortcuts on the desktop (see page 94) for the programs you want to startup automatically

2 Right-click Start, select Explore then click Startup in the Folders list

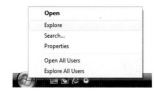

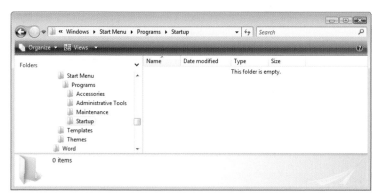

3 Drag the program shortcuts into the Startup folder (see page 68 for moving items to a folder)

4 The programs in the Startup folder (Paint and Calculator in our illustration) will now start automatically each time you start Windows

Hot tip

To open the Startup folder, you could click Start, All Programs and right-click the Startup entry and select Open.

Don't forget

If you drag a shortcut to a document file into the Startup folder, the associated program will start up with that document displayed, whenever you start up Windows.

Minimized (or Maximized)

Sometimes you may want to start a program but not use it right away. You, therefore, need to set it up so that when it's started it is minimized automatically. When you are ready to use the program, you only need to click on its task button on the Taskbar.

Hot tip

If you've added several programs to the Startup folder (see page 97), you can change the shortcuts in the Startup folder so they open minimized.

1 Create a shortcut for a program you want to start minimized (see page 94)

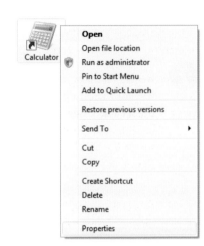

2 Right-click on the shortcut program icon and then select Properties from the menu

3 Click the Shortcut tab

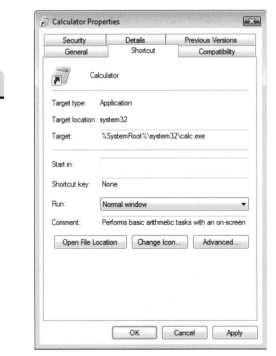

4 Click the down arrow for Run and select Minimized

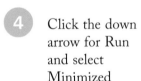

Don't forget

If you prefer to run a particular program in full window view, select Maximized in the Properties for the program shortcut.

5 Click OK to save the change

Install and Uninstall

If the program you want to install is provided on CD or DVD, you normally just insert the disc. The installation program starts up automatically and you can follow the instructions to select features and complete the installation.

If the installation does not start automatically, you can use the Run command to start the program manually (see page 92), or examine the contents of the disc using Windows Explorer.

To review your existing installed programs:

1. Select the Start button and then select Control Panel

Programs
Uninstall a program
Change startup programs

2. Select Uninstall a Program, in the Programs section, to display Uninstall or Change a Program

3. Select a program and you'll be offered options such as Uninstall, Change or Repair

4. Click View Installed Updates for a record of changes that have been applied

Hot tip

The installation program is often called Setup.exe or Install.exe, though this does vary from product to product.

Don't forget

If you have selected the Classic View for Control Panel, you would double-click Programs and Features.

Programs and Features

Beware

Some programs require you to insert the original program CD before you can continue, so make sure that the CDs are available.

Windows Features

There are numerous components in Windows, some of which are made available at installation time, while others are turned off. In earlier versions of Windows you were required to uninstall or reinstall Windows components. However, in this version, the features remain installed at all times, you just specify whether they should be active or not.

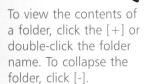

Don't forget

You may be prompted for an administrator password or for confirmation to proceed with this function.

1 Open the Uninstall or Change a Program option (see page 99) and click the option Turn Windows features on or off

2 To turn on a feature, click the associated box

3 To turn off a feature, clear its box

4 [+] means there is a subfolder with more features

Hot tip

To view the contents of a folder, click the [+] or double-click the folder name. To collapse the folder, click [-].

5 A filled box means that only some of the features are turned on

6 Click OK to confirm any changes

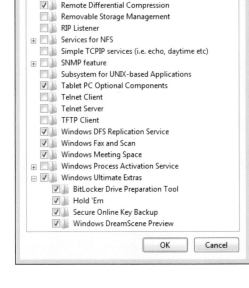

Tablet PC Components

The Windows features include optional components for the Tablet PC. This is a mobile PC with a touch sensitive screen that you can write on or interact with using a tablet pen or your finger. The components provided are:

- **Snipping Tool**
- **Sticky Notes**
- **Tablet PC Input Panel**
- **Windows Journal**

These are enabled even on standard PCs, where they can still be used. In particular, the Snipping Tool offers an easy way to capture a screenshot that can be pasted into a document or email.

1 With the required window visible, click Start, All Programs, Accessories then select the Snipping Tool

2 Click the arrow next to New and choose the snip method

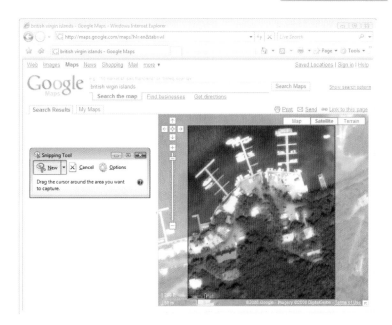

3 Click New and use the mouse to mark out the area of the screen or to select the particular window to capture

Beware

Tablet PC support is not included in the Windows Vista Home Basic edition.

Hot tip

Click Start and start typing Snipping, then select the Snipping Tool entry that appears at the top of the Start menu.

Programs
    Snipping Tool

Don't forget

You can capture a free-form area, a rectangle, a window or the whole of the display, as desired.

...cont'd

Hot tip

Select File, Save As to save the image in your Pictures folder as a .JPG, .PNG, .GIF or .MHT (single file HTML).

Don't forget

When you choose to send the snip as part of an email, your default email program will automatically be launched.

4 The snip is copied to the mark-up window, where you can highlight, annotate, save or share the snip

5 For example, click the arrow next to the Send Snip button to send the snip in an email (as an embedded or attached jpeg image)

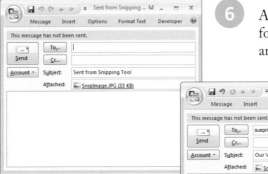

6 Add email addresses for the recipients, and edit the subject

7 Type the message and click the Send button to transmit the message

Select the Highlighter to emphasize parts of the image. If you are skillful with the mouse, click the Pen to annotate the image. There's no Undo function, but you can remove the annotations and highlighting with the Eraser.

Pen   Highlighter   Eraser

Program Compatibility

If you have an older program or a game that was written specifically for a previous version of Windows, it might run poorly or not at all under Windows Vista. If this is the case then:

1 Start the Program Compatibility Wizard from Help and Support and follow the instructions

> **Run the Program Compatibility Wizard**
>
> 1. → Click to open the Program Compatibility Wizard.

2 You'll be guided to locate the program, choose the level of Windows that best supports this program, then alter the display settings if appropriate

3 You'll be given the opportunity to try out the program. If the program worked, save the settings for future use

4 A Compatibility tab is added to the program Properties

Command Prompt

Windows includes an MS-DOS simulator in the form of the Command Prompt, which supports DOS commands and runs old DOS programs. To obtain the Command Prompt:

1 Click Start, All Programs, Accessories and then select Command Prompt

2 Type MS-DOS commands at the command line. To display a list of commands and a brief description, type Help and press Enter

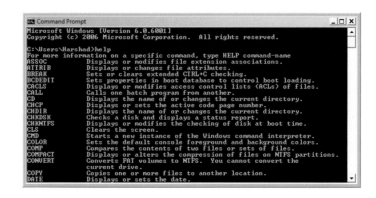

3 To set command prompt options, right-click the title bar and select Default (to change all Command Prompt Windows) or Properties (for just this window)

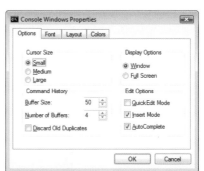

4 When you have finished, click on the Close (X) button or type EXIT and press the Enter key

---

Don't forget

Press Alt+Enter to make the Command Prompt window full-screen if it's windowed, or vice versa.

104

Hot tip

For more detailed help on a specific command, type Help followed by the command (or type Command /?).

You may need to select a specific folder to work with at the command prompt. You could use the MS-DOS commands to change folders. For example, to switch to user Harshad's Pictures folder you'd type: cd c:\users\harshad\pictures.

However, if the folder is already open and visible on your screen, there's a quick way to open the Command Prompt ready switched to that folder:

1 Hold down Shift as you right-click the folder, then select the entry Open Command Window Here from the extended menu that is displayed

2 The Command Prompt window appears, ready positioned at the required folder

Some commands will require administrator authority. To run these, open the Command Prompt as an administrator.

1 Click Start, All Programs, Accessories and then right-click Command Prompt and select Run as Administrator

Don't forget

The Open Command Window Here entry is hidden when you right-click a folder without pressing Shift.

Hot tip

The extended menu also provides the Copy as Path option which places the full path of the selected folder (or file) into the Clipboard.

Beware

This option will only be available for user accounts that have Administrator authority.

105

Quick Launch Toolbar

The Quick Launch toolbar may be hidden on your system. To make it appear on the taskbar:

1 Right-click the taskbar and select Toolbars then click Quick Launch

2 Click and drag program shortcuts from the desktop or the Start menu onto the Quick Launch toolbar

3 If there's a >> symbol on the toolbar, there are hidden entries. Click the symbol to reveal these shortcuts

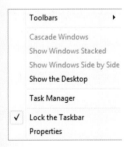

4 Drag the divider to extend the toolbar to show all the shortcuts on the Quick Launch toolbar

5 The first 10 icons are assigned Windows Logo key shortcuts WinKey+# (1 - 9 and 0 for the 10th)

Task Manager

Task Manager lists all the programs and processes running on your computer, you can monitor performance or close a program that is no longer responding. To open Task Manager:

1 Press Ctrl+Shift+Esc, or right-click the Taskbar and select Task Manager, to see the list of applications running

2 If an application is marked as Not Responding and you cannot wait for Windows to fix things, select the program and click End Task

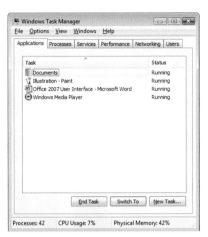

3 Click the Processes tab to show the process for the current user, or click the box Show processes from all users to see the complete list

4 You'll see many processes to support the active applications. In this case, the four tasks have 14 current user processes and 42 processes in total

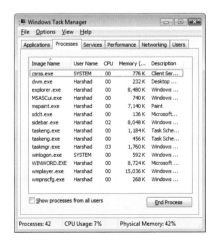

5 The total CPU time and the amount being used by each process are shown as (continually varying) percentages

6 Click the Performance tab to see graphs of resource usage

Don't forget

You can also press Ctrl+Alt+Delete, which displays the menu:
-> Lock this computer
-> Switch User
-> Log off
-> Change a password
-> Start Task Manager

Beware

If a program stops responding, Windows will try to find the problem and fix it automatically. Using Task Manager to end the program may be quicker, but any unsaved data will be lost.

...cont'd

Don't forget

If you have a local area network, there will also be a Networking tab, featuring a network usage graph.

Hot tip

Resize the window so it does not take up too much space on your screen, and you can see the effects on CPU and memory as you use your system.

⑦ The Performance panel shows graphs of the recent history of CPU and memory usage, along with other details

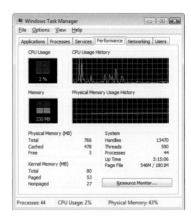

Alternative View

In addition to the standard view, with menus and tabs, Task Manager also has a CPU graph-only view.

① To switch to the other view double-click the graph area on the Performance tab

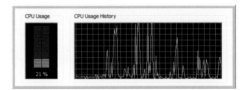

② To switch back to the view with menus and tabs, double-click the border of the Task Manager window

Resource Manager

① Click the Resource Monitor button for an even more detailed view of performance on your computer

7 Internet and Windows

New Internet Connection

Hot tip

Most ISPs also provide additional services such as email accounts, web servers and storage space on their Internet servers for you to create your own website.

Don't forget

It is usually better to use the software and procedures offered by your ISP, if possible, since they will be specifically tailored for the particular service.

Don't forget

Windows tries to detect and configure your connections automatically during installation, so you may find the connection is already established.

Before you can use the Internet and browse the web, your computer needs to be set up for connection to the Internet. To do this you'll require:

- An Internet Service Provider (ISP), to provide an account that gives you access to the Internet

- A transmission network – cable, telephone or wireless

- Some hardware to link into that transmission network

  For a broadband connection, such as Digital Subscriber Line (DSL) or cable, you need a DSL or Cable modem or router, usually provided by the ISP.

  For dial-up connection, you need a dial-up modem, which is usually pre-installed on your computer.

Your ISP may provide software to help you set up your hardware, configure your system and register your ISP account details. However, if you are required to install the connection or, if you are configuring a second connection as a backup, you can use the Windows Connect to the Internet wizard.

1. Click Start, Control Panel, View Network Status and Tasks (or in Classic View, double-click Network and Sharing Center)

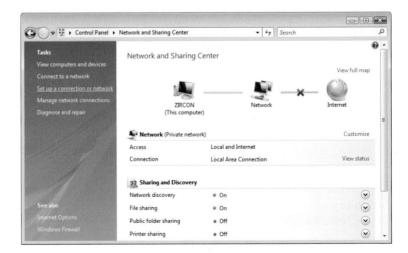

2 Click Setup a Connection or Network (see page 110) to display the connection options supported

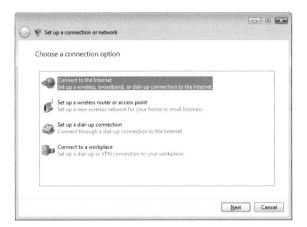

3 Select Connect to the Internet and click Next

Beware

If Windows has already recognized your connection, it detects this. You can select Browse the Internet now (see page 114) or set up a second connection (e.g. as a backup).

4 The New Connection Wizard launches. Select the appropriate connection method from those offered

Windows identifies all of the possible connection methods based on the hardware configuration of your computer. If you have a wireless router or network, you may have an option for Wireless connection. If there's no dial-up modem installed in your computer, then the Dial-up connection method will not be offered.

5   If you selected the broadband method of connection,
    you'll be asked to enter the user name and password that
    your ISP will have provided for you

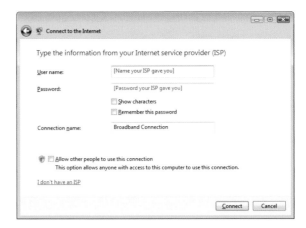

Don't forget

If you have another
computer that is already
connected to the
Internet, you can connect
the computer using a
local area network (see
page 160) and share
that connection with
your Windows Vista PC.

6   If you chose Dial-up, you will also be asked for a user
    name and password, the telephone number and the
    dialing rules for your location

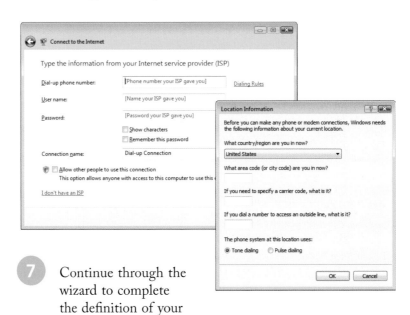

7   Continue through the
    wizard to complete
    the definition of your
    Internet connection, ready to start browsing the Internet

Start Internet Explorer

There are a number of ways to open Internet Explorer, though they may not all be enabled on your computer:

1 Double-click the Internet Explorer icon on the desktop

Internet Explorer

2 Click the Internet Explorer icon on the Quick Launch bar

3 Select Start and click Internet, at the top of the Start menu

4 There's a shortcut in Start, All Programs

The Internet Explorer window shares the features described for Windows Explorer (see page 48), including the hidden Menu bar, but there are some differences and some extra items:

Toolbar   Title bar   Address bar   Tabbed browsing
          (with title)   (with URL)   (multipage)

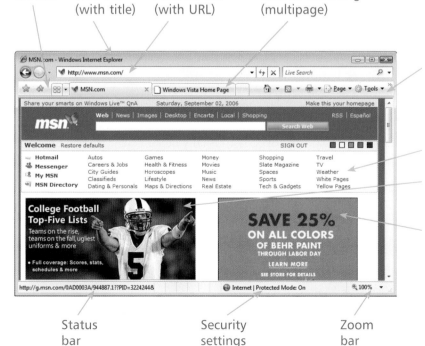

Command bar

Text hyperlinks

Graphical hyperlink

Advertisement

Status   Security   Zoom
bar   settings   bar

Don't forget

You can select Start, All Programs, Accessories, System Tools to find Internet Explorer (No Add-ons). This is a special troubleshooting version, for use when you have problems with particular websites.

Internet Explorer (No Add-ons)

Browse the Web

The World Wide Web (or Web for short) is an enormous collection of websites, each consisting of interconnected web pages. Every page on the web has a unique address, called a URL (Uniform Resource Locator) or simply a web address. You see these advertised everywhere – newspapers, magazines, television. The typical URL will look similar to this one:

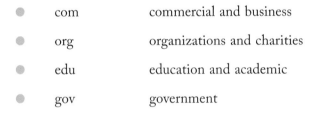

http://www.microsoft.com/windows/default.mspx

web page indicator	server name	site type	sub section	web page

Beware

Mistyping a URL can display sites that take advantage of common typing errors to parody genuine websites, so be very careful to type addresses exactly as supplied.

The server name is usually the company or organization name (in lower case), e.g. microsoft or ineasysteps.

The types of websites include:

- com   commercial and business
- org   organizations and charities
- edu   education and academic
- gov   government

There may also be a country suffix, for example:

- com.au   Australia
- ca   Canada
- co.uk   United Kingdom

To visit the main web page for a company or organization, the server name and site type will usually be sufficient as default values for the remaining parts will be assumed. For example, to address the main website for Microsoft, the URL address required is www.microsoft.com.

Don't forget

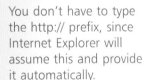

You don't have to type the http:// prefix, since Internet Explorer will assume this and provide it automatically.

To display a web page:

1 Click in the Address bar and begin to type the URL of the web page you want to visit

As you type an address, Internet Explorer tries to finish it, based on web pages you've visited before. If the page you want appears in the drop-down list, click that entry. Otherwise, continue typing until it does appear.

2 If no suggestion is offered, complete the address and click the Go To button or press Enter

Once you've reached a website, you can switch to another page, on the same site or on a different site, without typing a URL.

3 Move the mouse over a text or graphical hyperlink and the URL is displayed on the Status bar. Click to visit that address

Browser Buttons

There's no Menu bar displayed, and toolbar buttons have been re-arranged, for the Windows Vista version of Internet explorer.

The most useful browser buttons have been placed on the left of the window, alongside the Address bar.

Back and Forward
Click the back and forward buttons to switch between recently visited web pages, or click the down arrow to select an entry from the Recent Pages list

Favorites Center
View the lists of favorites, feeds, and the website history

Add to Favorites
Add the current web page to your Favorites list

Quick Tabs and Tab List
View multiple pages in the same Internet Explorer window

New Tab button
Add another concurrent web page

The Address bar

This includes the Go To, Stop and Refresh buttons to control the loading of the web page specified in the address box

The Search box
This provides the Search Options button that allows you to select your preferred search providers (see page 119)

The remaining toolbar buttons are incorporated into the Command bar on the right. By default, the following seven buttons are enabled:

	Home	Display the default Home web pages
	Feeds	View or subscribe to RSS feeds on the page
	Print	Print web page (includes scaling to fit)
	Page	Send page, send link, open in new window
	Tools	Pop up Blocker, Phishing Filter, manage add-ons
	Help	Contents and Index, Tour, support, feedback
	Research	Reference books, research sites, financial sites

Don't forget

You can adjust the length of the Command bar, to show more buttons. If Lock the Toolbars is enabled (ticked), click to unlock, then drag the toolbar handle at the left.

To change the buttons available, right-click the Command bar and select Customize Command Bar, then click Add or Remove Commands. The additional buttons available include:

	Read Mail	Start email program, e.g. Windows Mail
	Size	Choose text size (smallest to largest)
	Encoding	Choose an alternative language coding
	Edit	Toggle full screen view
	Cut	Copy to clipboard and remove
	Copy	Copy to clipboard, without removing
	Paste	Copy from clipboard
	Full Screen	Toggle full screen view on and off

Search the Internet

If you are looking for something, but don't have a web address, use the Internet Explorer search features to locate likely pages.

1 Click in the Instant Search box and type a word or phrase related to the topic, then press Enter

2 The search is completed using Windows Live Search and the matching web pages are listed, with brief outlines

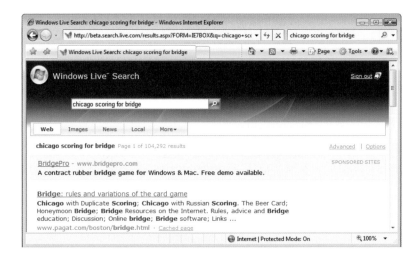

3 Click an entry to view the page. The Back button will return you to the Results list

Address bar searches

The Address bar also operates as a search box.

1 In the Address bar, type Find, Go or ? followed by the word or phrase and then press Enter (or Alt+Enter)

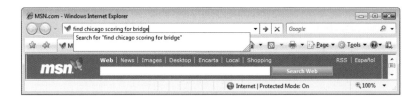

Change Search Provider

To add some new search providers to Internet Explorer:

1 Click the arrow at the right of the Search box, then click Find More Providers

2 The Internet Explorer search guide web page shows all the search providers supported

3 Select a provider, for example, Google and click the box Make this my default search provider, if desired. Then click Add Provider

4 To choose a different search provider, just for the current session, click the arrow to open the Search options and select the one you want

5 To make a change to the default, you'd click Change Search Defaults and select your preferred search provider

Hot tip

You can add extra search providers, for example Lycos and Yahoo, without making a change to the default and have them listed in Search options, ready for use when required.

119

Hot tip

To remove all added search providers and return to the original choice, click Change Search Defaults and press the Restore Defaults button.

Bookmark Favorites

If you see a web page that you want to revisit, add it to your Favorites list to save having to record or remember the address.

1 While viewing the page, click the Add to Favorites button and then click the Add to Favorites menu entry (or press Ctrl+D)

2 The page title is used as the name for the new favorite, but you can type an alternative name if you wish

3 Click Add to save the details in your Favorites list

View Favorites

1 Click the Favorites Center button and click the Favorites button (if not already selected)

2 Click on a folder name to expand it

3 Click any Favorites entry to display that web page

4 Click Add to Favorites and Organize Favorites, to move, rename or delete entries from the list

RSS Feeds

RSS (Really Simple Syndication) Feeds provide the frequently updated content from a news or blog website. Internet Explorer can discover and display feeds as you visit websites, or you can subscribe to feeds to automatically check for and download updates that you can view later.

Discover a Feed

1 Open Internet Explorer and browse to a website that has feeds. The Feeds button changes color to let you know

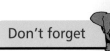

2 Click the Feeds button to see the list of feeds available, for example at the CNN website (www.cnn.com)

CNN - Top Stories [RSS]
CNN - Recent Stories [RSS]

3 Click one of the feeds to view the contents and you are offered the opportunity to subscribe, so that feed updates will be automatically downloaded to your computer

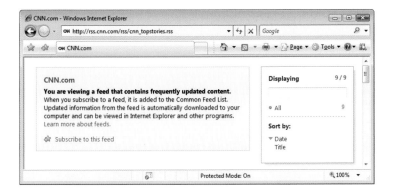

4 Click Subscribe to this Feed, then click the Subscribe button, to add the feed to your list in the Favorites Center

Hot tip

If you click the Feed button, you'll select the first in the list (or the only feed if there's just one offered).

Don't forget

To view your subscribed feeds, click the Favorites Center button and then select the Feeds button.

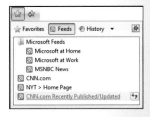

History

Hot tip

You can also press
Ctrl+H to open the
Favorites Center at the
History section.

1 Open the Favorites Center and click the History button

2 Pin the Favorites Center to the window (see page 120), so you can browse the History entries

3 Click the down arrow next to the History button, to change the sort order for the entries

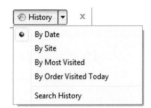

Manage the History

1 Select Tools, Internet Options and click the General tab

Don't forget

The general Internet
Options also cover Home
Page, Search, Tabs and
appearance settings (see
page 123).

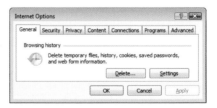

2 At Browsing History, click Delete to remove the records, or Settings to change the history period (default 20 days)

Home Page

Your home page is displayed when you start Internet
Explorer or when you click the Home button. The
web page displayed may be the Windows default,
may have been defined by your ISP or your computer supplier.
However, you can choose any web page as your home page.

Current web page

1 With the preferred web page
displayed in the current tab,
click the arrow next to the
Home button and select Add
or Change home page

2 Use this page as your
only home page or add
the page to your set of
home pages

Hot tip

You can define all the
open browser tabs as
your home page (see
page 124).

Reset home page

1 Click Tools, Internet Options and click the General tab

2 Click Use Default to
use the home page
specified when you
installed Internet
Explorer

or

Click Use Blank
to start up with no
home page, e.g.
when using the
computer offline

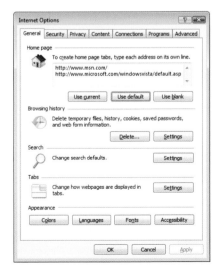

Don't forget

You can specify a new
home page by typing
the web address into the
home page box.

3 Click OK to save the
changes

Tabbed Browsing

You can open multiple websites in a single browser window, with each web page on a separate tab.

1 To open a blank tab, click the New Tab button

2 Scroll down and click Close to clear the tab

3 To switch between tabs, click the page tab on the tab row or click the Quick Tabs button and select the page

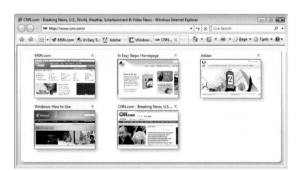

4 When you close Internet Explorer you are asked if you want to close all tabs. Click Show Options, and select Open these next time, if you need to continue working with the same set of web pages

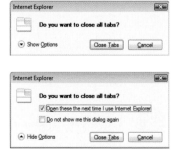

Hot tip

Click in the box Don't show this page again, and the New Tab button will display a clear tab immediately.

Don't forget

To open a web page link in a new tab, press Ctrl as you click or right-click the link and select Open in New Tab.

Hot tip

To save the group of tabs, click Add to Favorites (see page 120) and select Add tab group to Favorites.

Zoom

Internet Explorer Zoom allows you to enlarge or reduce your view of a web page. Unlike the Size button (see page 117), it enlarges everything on the page, images and text.

1 Click the Zoom button to view the page at 125%, 150% or 200% (it selects the next value, each time you click)

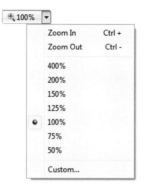

2 Click the down arrow to select one of the predefined zoom levels (for example, 200%)

Hot tip

Reduce (zoom out) to get an overall view of a large web page. Enlarge (zoom in) to see the fine detail for one section of the page.

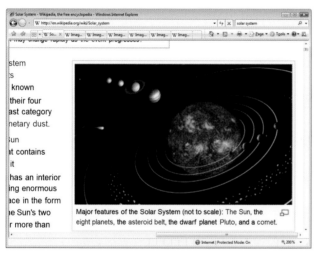

Major features of the Solar System (not to scale): The Sun, the eight planets, the asteroid belt, the dwarf planet Pluto, and a comet.

3 Click the Zoom button once, to return to 100%

Wheel Mouse Zoom

1 If you have a wheel mouse, hold down Ctrl and scroll the wheel to zoom in or out

Keyboard zoom

1 Press Ctrl - to reduce, or Ctrl + to enlarge, in 10% increments. Press Ctrl 0 to return to 100%

Print

When you click the 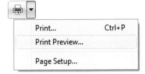 button on the Command bar, Internet Explorer automatically prints the web page on the current tab. The print is automatically scaled to fit the paper size so that you won't find the right-hand edge chopped off, as often happened in previous releases.

Use Print Preview to see how the printed web page will appear.

1 With the required web page open, click the arrow next to the print button and select Print Preview

2 Note the Shrink to Fit option preselected in the Change Print Size box

3 To illustrate the benefit of this, click the down arrow and select 100% to see how the print image is truncated

Hot tip

Click the Portrait or Landscape buttons to quickly reorientate the print image. For larger web pages, you can preview up to 12 print pages, to see how the complete web page will be presented.

Don't forget

You can select a print zoom factor from 30% to 200%, or enter a custom value. Full page view also provides easy to adjust margin handles.

8 Email and Windows

Windows allows you to send and receive email messages online, using Internet Explorer on any computer. You can also use Windows Mail to download and store your email messages on your own computer and take advantage of security functions such as spam blocking and phishing filters.

Web Mail

Web Mail stores and retains your email on a mail server. To access your messages, you connect to the Internet and use Internet Explorer (or another web browser).

1 Open Internet Explorer and visit the website for your web mail provider, e.g. www.gmail.com

2 Provide your account name (usually your email ID or the full email address) and your password, then click Sign in

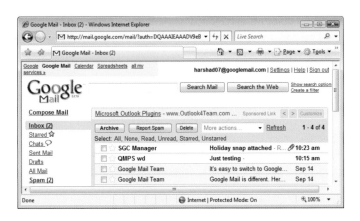

3 You'll see a list of headers with details such as sender, subject and date or time. There may also be a paperclip icon to indicate that there are files attached

4 Double click a message header to open it, enabling the contents of the message to be retrieved from the server and displayed. The message remains on the server, unless you explicitly delete it

Hot tip

To delete messages, click in the boxes to select the messages, then click the Delete button to remove them from the server.

As a result, the messages can be viewed again, from any computer connected to the Internet. This is very useful if you want to check mail from other locations, for example, at an Internet cafe while on vacation, from a laptop and from a desktop computer.

The disadvantage is that you must be connected to the Internet and signed on to the email account, for any actions involving messages. The retrieval process may also be time consuming.

POP Mail

POP Mail also stores messages on the mail server, but when you retrieve your mail, using Windows Mail (or another email application), the messages are transferred from the server to the computer issuing the request. When the transfer is completed, the messages are deleted from the server.

You will be able to read messages and compose replies without having to be connected to the Internet. You may also have functions and features that are not available via web mail, such as message or diary management. Message access will often be much faster. However, once you have downloaded your mail, you must have access to that computer to view the messages again.

POP – Post Office Privacy

129

Hot tip

Most web mail providers have a POP mail facility, so you can use both methods with the same account. However, there may be a charge for this service in some cases. Similarly, your ISP may provide web access to your POP email account.

Enable Pop Mail

If your email account is web-based, like the Gmail accounts from Google, your messages are stored on the mail server, managed by your email service supplier. This means you must always be online to read your messages. However, you may be able to change the settings for the account so that you can download your messages and store them on your computer, using the POP mail function. This requires an application such as Windows Mail (or Outlook Express).

To enable POP in your Gmail account:

 Log in to your Gmail account and click Settings at the top of the web page

harshad07@googlemail.com | Settings | Help | Sign out

 Click the Forwarding and POP tab in Mail Settings

 Beware

This step will not be necessary for email accounts provided as a POP service by your ISP.

 Select Enable POP for all mail (to download existing messages) or Enable POP for mail that arrives from now on

 Choose what action to take with Gmail messages after they are accessed with POP

Your preferences have been saved.

Start Windows Mail

Windows Mail provides the tools that you require in order to send and receive email messages using the POP mail method.

To start Windows Mail:

1 Click Start and then click the Email entry at the top of the Start menu

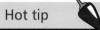

Hot tip

Previous versions of Windows provided Outlook Express to support the email functions. In Windows Vista, this is replaced by Windows Mail.

2 The first time you start Windows Mail, it will prompt you for your email account details, beginning with your name

Don't forget

The email service provider may offer an automatic method for defining your account details to the email program, to save you entering the details manually.

3 Next, you will need to provide your email address (ID and server name, separated by the @ symbol)

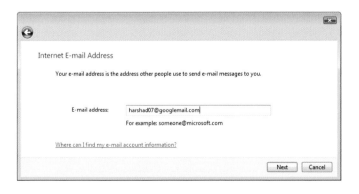

...cont'd

4 Specify the incoming and outgoing email servers for your service provider. For Gmail, you'd put:

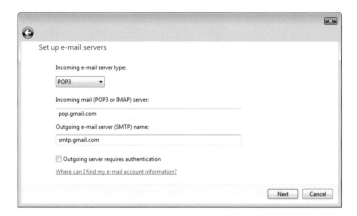

5 Your account name (usually the email ID or address) and the associated password are required

6 This completes the account definition, but you may have some additional security settings, depending on your ISP

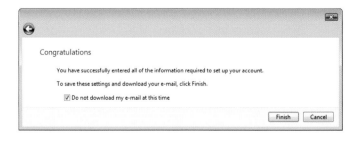

Security Settings

If your ISP requires particular security settings for the email account, you'll need to adjust its properties.

1. To list the Internet accounts defined in your Windows Mail, select Tools, Accounts

2. Select your new email account and click the Properties button

3. Gmail requires you to specify the server port numbers. These can be found on the Advanced tab

Don't forget

In addition to email accounts, Windows Mail supports newsgroup accounts (see page 140).

Beware

Only change these settings if your ISP tells you that the servers require a secure connection (SSL) and provides the necessary port numbers.

...cont'd

4 In many cases, the ISP may say that the outgoing server requires authentication. This option is on the Servers tab

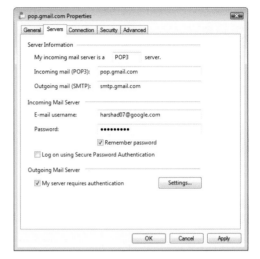

Hot tip

If you use a different account for sending email and for receiving email, then you'll need to provide the specific logon details for that account.

5 To check the action, click the Settings button. Normally, you'd use the same logon details as the incoming server

6 You are now ready to click Send/Receive to download any messages that are waiting (see page 135)

Don't forget

You'll require a connection to the Internet (dial-up or DSL or cable) just as for Internet Explorer (see page 110).

Receive Emails

1 Open Windows Mail and click the Send/Receive button

Don't forget

You must be connected to the Internet, by dial-up or by broadband, in order to be able to send or receive messages.

2 Note that the currently selected message will be displayed in the preview pane, and automatically marked as read

3 To switch off the Preview pane, select View and click the Layout entry

4 Clear the box that is labeled Show preview pane

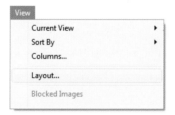

Beware

The message that is automatically selected and displayed could turn out to be spam, so it might be better to avoid using the preview pane.

Read a Message

Downloaded messages are stored in your Inbox. The sender, the title and the date/time sent are displayed along with icons that indicate the status of the messages:

 The closed yellow envelope indicates an Unread message

 The open white envelope indicates a Read message

 The paperclip icon indicates a file Attachment

 The blue down arrow indicates a Low priority message

 The red exclamation mark is for a High priority message

Hot tip

The envelope icons are changed to indicate when you have replied to a message (see page 137) or forwarded it to another email address.

1. Select the Inbox folder and the message you want to read, then press Enter or double-click the message header

Beware

Previous just means higher in the list of messages, so if they are sorted in chronological order – newest at the top, the Previous messages will actually be newer.

2. The message opens in its own window. Scroll through the message (if necessary) to see all the content

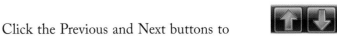

3. Click the Previous and Next buttons to view the other messages in the list

Reply to a Message

It is easy to respond to any email message that you receive.

1 With the message open, click the Reply button to send an answer to the originator

Hot tip

Click Reply All to send the message to all recipients of the email, as well as to the originator.

2 Note the Re: prefix that gets added to the message subject. Type the response above the original message text

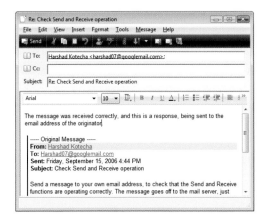

3 Click the File Attachment button or the Priority button, if appropriate

4 Click the Send button, and the reply will be placed in the Outbox

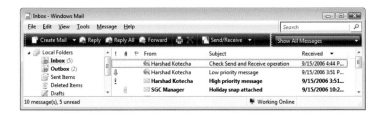

Don't forget

If you are connected to the Internet, the reply message will be sent immediately and then transferred from the Outbox to the Sent Items folder. If you are offline, replies will be sent the next time you press Send/Receive.

5 The envelope icons are modified to show that a response to the message has been sent

Compose a New Message

1 Click the Create Mail button to open a plain message form

or

click the down arrow and select one of the stationery types (these give decorative background patterns for the message form)

2 A fresh message form is displayed

Beware

If there are more than one entry in your Windows Contacts (see page 139) that could satisfy the name typed so far, you'll get a list of possible names and addresses to choose from.

Hot tip

Click the To: button or the Cc: button, and select entries directly from the list in your Windows Contacts.

3 Start typing a recipient name, then click the Check Names button. The associated email address will be inserted

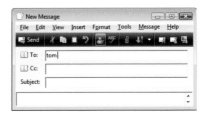

4 Enter additional names as required, then complete and send the message (as described for a reply to a message, page 137)

Windows Contacts

1 Open a Windows Mail message from the particular person or group, and right-click the sender name

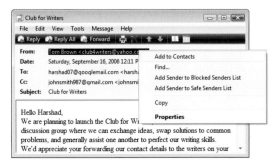

2 Click Add to Contacts, enter any additional details that you have, e.g. phone number, mailing address and even a photograph or image, then click OK

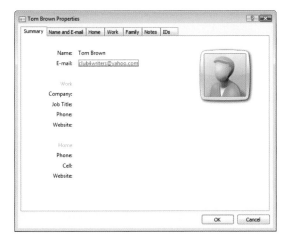

3 To open your Windows Contacts folder, select Start, click your user name and choose the Contacts folder

139

Newsgroups

Newsgroups are Internet discussion forums, international in scope, where users with common interests exchange views and information. Unlike email messages, visible only to the sender and the specified recipients, newsgroup messages can be read by anyone who views the group that they're posted to.

Newsgroups require a newsreader program to download messages from a news server. This function is included in Windows Mail. Your ISP may provide news servers, and there are many private news servers and newsgroups that require an account name and password for access. There's also a predefined link to the Microsoft newsgroups.

Hot tip

At any time, you can press Ctrl+W in Windows Mail to display the list of newsgroups that already have been downloaded.

1 Open Windows Mail and select Tools, Newsgroups

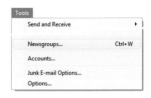

2 The list of newsgroups available is downloaded. This is only needed the first time you access the newsgroups

3 There are many hundreds of newsgroups, so type a term to focus the list

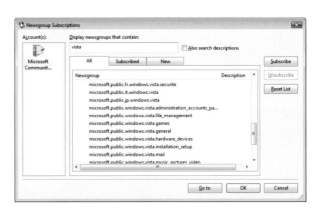

Don't forget

When you select to search descriptions, you may be required to download the list again, since the descriptions are not initially included.

4 To help locate specific newsgroups, click the box Also search descriptions

Subscribe to a newsgroup

It can be tedious to search for newsgroups to check for the latest updates, so it may be worth subscribing to particular newsgroups. These will then be available on the Windows Mail folder list, and you can have the latest messages downloaded automatically.

1 Display the list of newsgroups (see page 140)

2 Click the particular news server, if there's more than one, that contains the newsgroup you'd like to subscribe to

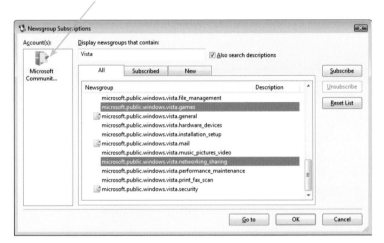

Don't forget

A folder icon will appear next to any newsgroups you have subscribed to.

141

Hot tip

To subscribe to more than one newsgroup, press the Ctrl key, then click the newsgroups you want to subscribe to.

3 Click the particular newsgroup, and then click Subscribe

4 Click OK to save your changes, and the newsgroups are added to the folder list ready for synchronizing

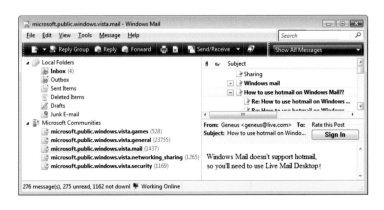

Block Spam Senders

Windows Mail helps you to keep your Inbox free of unsolicited commercial email messages (spam) by moving them to the Junk Email folder.

To specify the level of protection that you require:

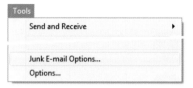

1 Select Tools and click Junk E-mail Options

Don't forget

Windows Mail will also protect your email from potential phishing attacks.

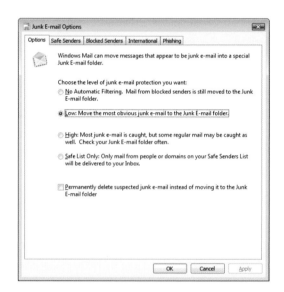

2 Choose No Automatic Filtering to stop blocking junk email messages. However, Windows Mail will still block messages from locations on your Blocked Senders list

3 Low blocks only the most obvious junk email and is sufficient if your account isn't particularly subject to spam

Beware

For High or Safe List Only, be sure to review the Junk email folder periodically, to detect if any legitimate email messages are moved there by mistake.

4 High may be necessary, if you receive a large volume of junk email messages

5 The Safe List Only is the most restrictive. You only receive messages from people or domain names on your Safe Senders list

If a legitimate email message has been blocked:

1 Open Windows Mail, click the Junk email folder, select the message that was misclassified

2 Select Message, Junk email, and then Mark as Not Junk. The message is moved to your Inbox

Beware

Marking a message as not junk will move that message to your Inbox, but future messages from that sender might still end up in the Junk email folder.

3 To prevent problems in the future, add the Sender to the Safe Senders List, using the same Junk Email menu

Don't forget

If you've already marked the message as not junk, you need to go to the Inbox, select the message and then add the sender to the safe list.

4 In a similar fashion, when a spam message gets through to the Inbox, select the message and choose Message, Junk Email, Add Sender to Blocked Senders List

When a message is received from an email address that's on the Blocked Senders list, it is automatically moved to the Junk email folder. However, if the address is also on the Safe Senders list, the message won't be treated as junk because the Safe Senders list has priority over the Blocked Senders list.

Send a Web Page

Hot tip

You could also click the Page button in Internet Explorer, select Send Page by Email or Send Link by Email, to open a new message in Windows Mail.

If you come across a web page that has information you'd like to share with others, you can send the contents in an email message.

1 With the web page open in Internet Explorer, click the Address bar, and copy (Ctrl+C) the URL to the clipboard

2 Open Windows Mail, click the arrow next to the Create Mail button, then select Web Page

3 Paste the web page URL into the Send Web Page box and click OK

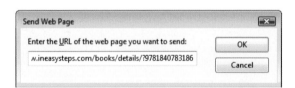

4 A new message form opens, with the web page contents. Add the recipient's address and the subject line, optionally insert a text note, then Send the message

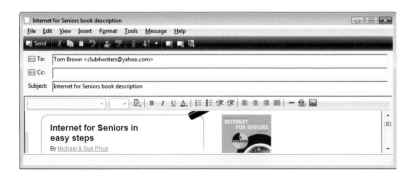

9 Fonts and Printing

You use many different fonts to display application documents, information from the web or your email messages. You'll need the same fonts or your printer's equivalent fonts, when you want to produce copies on a local or network printer.

Windows Fonts

Windows comes with about 200 different fonts. They provide a wide range of distinctive and artistic effects in Windows screens and documents, allowing support for a number of languages and for many special symbols.

To view the fonts available on your system:

 Select Start, Control Panel, Appearance and Personalization then click Fonts

The Fonts folder is displayed in Windows Explorer

Most of the Windows fonts will be TrueType or OpenType fonts which can be scaled to any size and can be sent to any printer or other output device that is supported by Windows. You may also have PostScript fonts (if required for your printer).

Preview Font

1 Open the Font folder, select the font and double-click (or just press Enter)

2 Examples of the font in use are displayed, in the form of a pangram (a sentence with all the letters of the alphabet) and the numerals, in various sizes up to 72 point

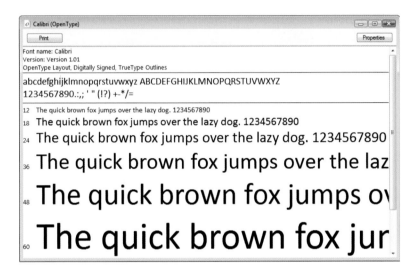

3 Some of the TrueType fonts are provided as collections. Click the forward or back arrows to view individual fonts

147

Character Map

As well as letters and numbers, the fonts contain many special characters, not all of which appear on your computer keyboard. You can insert these characters into your documents using the Character Map, or by pressing particular key combinations.

1 Select Start, All Programs, Accessories, System Tools, and then Character Map

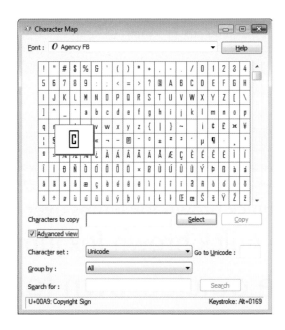

2 Click any character to see an enlarged version. The key combination is shown on the status bar, where relevant

3 Click Select to add the character to the copy box, and click Copy to transfer selected characters to the clipboard

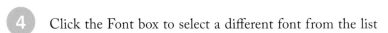

4 Click the Font box to select a different font from the list

Install New Fonts

1 Locate a useful font on the Internet, for example the Christmas Card font from www.wtv-zone.com/marciasuz/TTF/Holiday/ChristmasFonts.html (capitals required) and download the font file (ChristmasCardIAWL.ttf)

Hot tip

If you have a new font, supplied with an application or downloaded from the Internet, you must add it to your Fonts folder, unless the application has already done so.

2 Open the Fonts folder and select File, Install New Font

Beware

This action, using the File command, requires the Menu bar (see page 38). If you don't see the File menu, press the Alt key.

3 Select the drive and folder where you stored the font file, select the font and click Install

4 The font will be added to the Fonts folder, ready for use in any Windows application

Don't forget

To uninstall fonts, open the Fonts folder, select the fonts and delete them as you'd delete any files (see page 74).

ClearType Smoothing

ClearType is a mechanism to make on-screen text more detailed so that it appears clear and smooth and, easier to read for long periods of time without eye strain or fatigue.

ClearType is turned on by default in Windows. But if for any reason it's turned off, you can turn it back on.

To turn on ClearType:

1 Right-click the desktop and select Personalize

2 Click Windows Color and Appearance

3 Click the Effects button in the Appearance dialog box

4 Select Use the following method to smooth edges of screen fonts, choose ClearType and OK

This shows a piece of text (using the Cambria italic font at 14 point), captured from a Notepad window, before and after the ClearType smoothing was applied. The captured image has been magnified to emphasize the effect.

Add a Local Printer

In most cases Windows will automatically install the software that will allow it to work on your computer. To add a local printer, directly attached to your computer:

1 Connect the printer to the computer and switch the printer on (note: for parallel cable connections, you should shut down the computer before you attach the printer)

2 Restart the computer, if required, and Windows will automatically detect the printer and start adding software

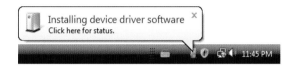

3 After a few moments, Windows should tell you that the device is installed and ready for use

4 To check the printer definition, select Start, Control Panel and select the Printer link

Hardware and Sound
Printer
Mouse

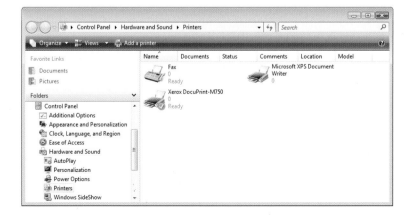

Beware

If your printer supplier has provided you with printer management software, this needs to be installed before you attach the printer to your computer.

Don't forget

This assumes you are using a printer which will be automatically recognized. This applies to most modern printers, and to all USB connected printers.

Hot tip

To open the Printers folder, you could also press the Windows logo key, type "printer" and select the Printers entry that appears at the top of the Start menu.

Add a Network Printer

1 Open the Printers folder (see page 151) and click the Add a Printer button on the Command bar

2 Select Add a Network Printer (no need to click Next). If your printer is listed, select it from the list, otherwise click The printer that I want isn't listed

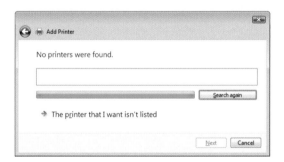

3 Select the printer by computer name and printer name (or click Browse to locate all the printers on the network)

4 The printer wizard will connect to the specified printer and install the driver software

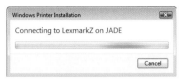

5 A suitable name is suggested and the printer is marked as the default. Modify this if desired then click Next

Don't forget

Clear the Set as the default printer box if you want to retain the existing setting for the default printer.

6 The printer will be added to your printer folder. Click the Print a test page button to check it out

Beware

Make sure that the network printer is switched on before sending it any print jobs.

153

7 The network attached printer will now appear in your Printers folder, along with the other printers

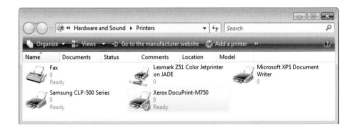

Print a Document

Once your printer is set up in Windows, you can print your document from the associated application, or drag the file onto the printer icon in the Printers folder.

From the Application

1 Open the document in the application program that was used to build it

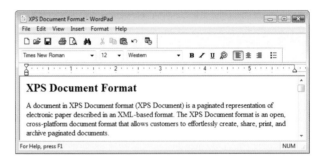

Don't forget

Click on the print button on the toolbar to quickly print one copy of the whole document to your default printer, without the need for the Print dialog box.

2 Select File, Print from the Menu bar, or press the Ctrl+P key combination

3 The default printer is selected, but you can change to any of the available printers

Hot tip

Click Preferences to change other print options for the selected documents, such as paper orientation, quality settings and color.

4 Amend the print options as required, e.g. Page Range or Number of copies, then click the Print button

Use Drag and Drop

1 Drag the file icon for the document you want to print

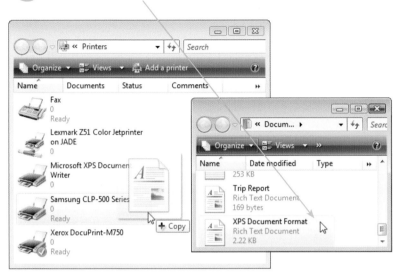

See page 82 for more information about file types and program associations.

2 Position the icon over the printer you want to use, then release the mouse button

When you drag and drop a file onto the printer icon, the program for that file type is started and, printing completes automatically.

Print to Shortcut
To make it easier to locate the printer, create a shortcut icon for the specific printer on the desktop.

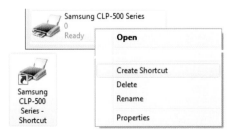

1 Right-click the printer icon and select Create Shortcut. The shortcut is added to the desktop

Print Preview

You can see what the print copy of your document will look like, without actually printing it to paper, if the application you are using offers the print preview function.

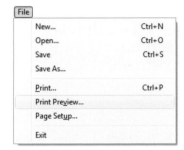

1 In the application window, select File, Print Preview

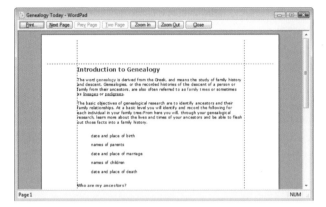

Don't forget

The Print Preview in some applications allows you to adjust print options (see page 126 for an example using Internet Explorer). In WordPad, you must use the Page Setup option.

2 You can view all the pages one or two at a time, zoom in and out, and print the documents

3 Close the preview and select File, Page Setup to make changes to the document layout

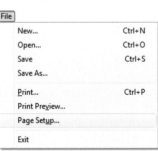

4 Click OK to apply the changes, then select File, Print

Print Management

When you submit a document for printing, Windows usually spools it to a temporary disk file rather than sending it directly to the printer. You can send several files for printing at once. They will be queued (spooled) in succession for your selected printer. This allows you to intercept and control their output from the print queue before they are physically printed.

Don't forget

You can also open the printer queue by double-clicking the small printer icon in the notification area, after a print job is submitted.

1 Double-click the printer icon in the Printers folder or the printer shortcut, to open the Printer queue

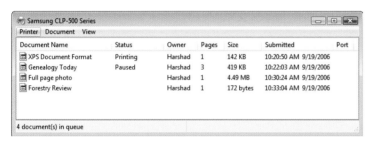

2 Select the name of the document you want to change the status of, and click Document on the menu bar. You can also right-click the document name to display a similar menu

Beware

Print jobs may be quickly transferred from the spool file to the memory on the printer, so select Printer, Pause Printing, to hold all jobs, when you want to work with the print queue.

From the menu, you can:

- Pause — Halt printing for the selected document (pages already sent to printer memory still continue)

- Resume — Continue printing of a paused document

- Restart — Print the document from the beginning

- Cancel — Remove the document from the print queue

- Properties — Change print options such as Schedule times and Priority (up to 99, the default being 1)

Hot tip

To change the status of several documents at once, hold down Ctrl and click each document in turn, right-click one of them and choose the option to apply to all the selected documents.

Printer Configuration

You can configure various printer settings to apply to all the documents that you print, changing things like paper size, print quality, and color management. The exact options offered will depend on the model of printer you have installed and on its class (e.g. local or network connected).

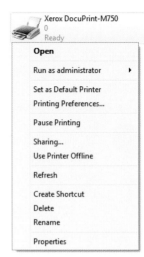

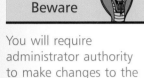
1 Right-click the icon for the Printer you want to configure, to display the menu

2 Click the Properties entry

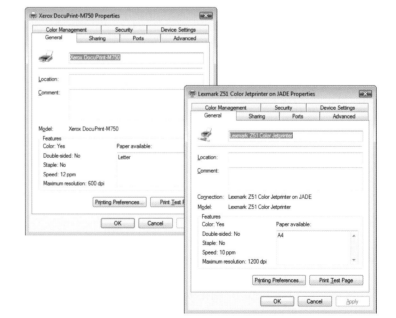

3 Click the Printing Preferences button on the General tab to change layout and paper specifications

Printing Preferences...

4 Select another tab and change settings as required, then click OK to apply all the changes

10 Networking

There is a built-in networking capability within Windows, allowing you to share files, printers and your Internet connection between two or more computers.

Network Components

There are numerous possibilities for setting up a home network. To start with, there are two major network technologies:

- Wired – e.g. Ethernet, using twisted pair cables, to send data at rates of 10, 100 or 1000 Mbps (megabits per second)

- Wireless – using radio waves to send data between computers, at rates of 11, 54 or 108 Mbps

There is also a variety of hardware items needed:

- Network adapter – appropriate to the network type, with one for each computer in the network

- Network controller – one or more hub, switch or router, providing the actual connection to each network adapter

Don't forget

The network adapter can be connected to the USB port, inserted in the PC Card slot or installed inside your computer.

Don't forget

Ethernet adapters connect to a network hub, switch or wired router. Wireless adapters connect through a wireless router or a combination of router/switch.

Hot tip

You may already have some of these elements in operation, if you have an existing network running a previous version of Windows.

160

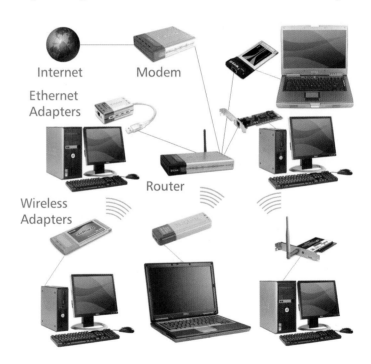

Internet   Modem

Ethernet Adapters

Router

Wireless Adapters

There's also the Internet connection (dial-up, DSL or cable) using:

- A modem connected to one of the computers

- A modem connected to the network

- Internet access incorporated into the router or switch

Set Up Your Network

The steps you'll need, and the most appropriate sequence to follow, will depend on the specific options on your system. However, the main steps will include:

- Install network adapters in the computers, where necessary

- Set up or verify the Internet connection

- Set up the wireless router or access point (wireless networks)

- Connect the computers and start up Windows on each PC

Install Hardware

If you need to install a wired or wireless network adapter, follow the instructions provided with the adapter. For example, to install the D-Link Wireless USB adapter:

1 Insert the CD provided and the setup program will start up automatically. Click the Install Driver option

2 Follow the instructions (giving permission for access where requested) to complete the software installation

3 Shut down and turn off the computer, then attach the USB adapter to the USB cable and cable to a USB port

4 Restart the computer. The USB adapter will be detected and the driver software enabled

5 You may see a message in the notification area, indicating that the network definition is incomplete. This is usually because, at this stage, not all components have been set up

Currently connected to:

Unidentified network
Access: Local only

3:10 PM

Don't forget

For how to connect a computer to the Internet see page 110.

Beware

If you go to a website that stays relatively static, some of its web pages might be stored on your computer and will display correctly even if your connection is faulty.

Internet Connection

You don't actually require an Internet connection to set up a network, if all you want to do is share files and printers. However, in most cases the main purpose of the network is to share your connection to the Internet across several computers.

Verify your Connection

If you already have an Internet connection, open your web browser and go to a website that gets regularly updated (e.g. a news site). If the website opens with up to date entries and you don't get any error messages your connection is working.

Install Router

You can use a router with a DSL modem (an Internet gateway) to make an Internet connection available for sharing. This is usually set up on one computer, connected via an Ethernet cable or a USB cable. A configuration program may be provided on an installation CD or you can use your web browser.

1 Open the browser and enter the IP address provided for the router, e.g. 192.168.1.1 or a similar local IP address

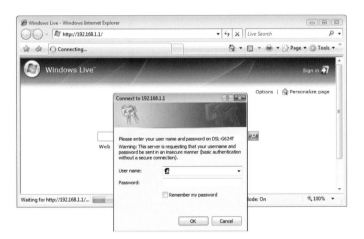

2 This will open an administrator sign on screen. Enter the user name and password provided

You'll be using the default ID and password for the particular equipment. While this can only be accessed from a direct local connection, you may feel more secure if you use the tools provided to change the password (and also change the ID, if allowed).

3   This will allow you to adjust the settings for the router, check status, use the tools and obtain help

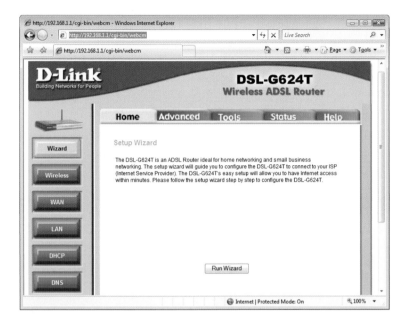

Don't forget

The options offered will depend on the particular features of your router or gateway device, but they should be similar in principle.

4   Click Run Wizard to use the Setup wizard to define the DSL, LAN and Wireless parameters for your network

5   For example, you will be able to specify the SSID (Service Set Identifier) and the encryption key for the wireless network

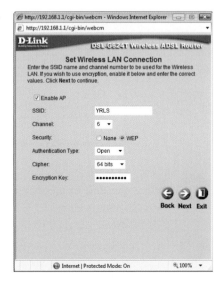

Beware

Do not use the default values for the parameters since these could be known to other people.

6   Select Restart to apply the changes and reboot the router

Discover Networks

Connect your computers to form your network, using Ethernet or HPNA cables and adapters or, by setting up your wireless adapters and routers. When you start up each of the computers, Windows Vista will examine the current configuration and discover any new networks that have been established since the last start up.

1 When a new network is detected, Windows asks you the location type – Home, Work or Public Location

2 Click the link to view or change settings in the Network and Sharing Center

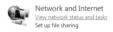

3 Another way to open this is to select Start, Network and then click the Network and Sharing Center button

Network and Sharing Center

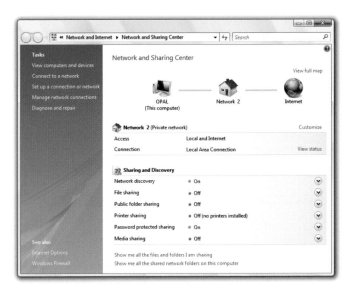

Don't forget

The Network and Sharing Center displays the network settings for the computer.

1 Click Customize to change the network name or location

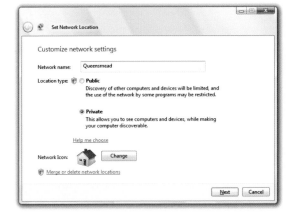

Beware

You should also turn off password protected sharing to give other users, without accounts on this computer, the opportunity to access shared resources.

2 Click the File Sharing button in the Network and Sharing Center to turn on file sharing

Network Map

1 Click View Full Map to see a schematic diagram of the networks detected, in this case Ethernet and wireless

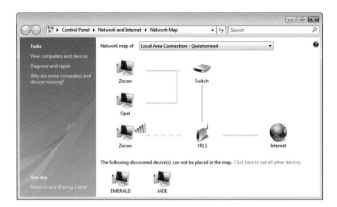

2 Click View computers and devices or Click here to see all other devices, and the Network folder opens

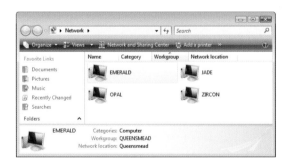

3 Double-click a computer icon, to see the resources that it is able to offer for sharing

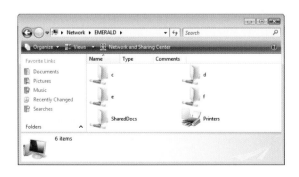

Share Files and Folders

1 Open the drive and select the folder you want to share

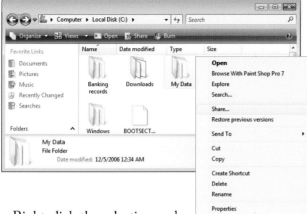

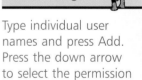

Hot tip

You can select a group of files and/or folders this way and share them all at once.

2 Right click the selection and click the Share option

Don't forget

Type individual user names and press Add. Press the down arrow to select the permission level, which can be either Reader, Contributor or Co-owner.

3 Click the Share button to share the selected folder with the specified users on the network

Beware

User names that have shared access to folders must have a password assigned.

Map to Shared Folder

1 Open the Computer folder and click the Map Network Drive button

2 Select a drive letter from the list of unused drive letters and type the path for the shared folder, or click the Browse button to select the computer and folder names

168

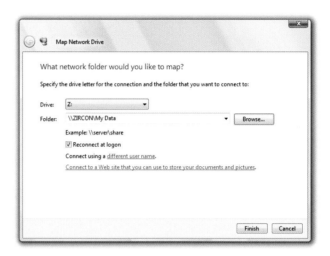

3 Select Reconnect at logon, to map to the folder every time you sign on to this computer, then click Finish

The shared folder appears in Computer, as a virtual drive.

11 Customize Windows

This chapter shows you how to change your Windows Vista desktop and alter other settings to suit your requirements. It also introduces the advanced visual capabilities of Aero, including transparency, Flip 3D and Live Windows Preview. You can create new user accounts and customize each one individually.

Personalize Your Computer

Add a personal touch to your computer by taking advantage of the flexibility in Windows, and personalize settings for your user name, to suit your preferences.

There are several ways to display the personalization options in Windows Vista:

1. Right-click the desktop and select the Personalize entry

2. Select Start, Control Panel and, with Classic View selected, double-click the Personalization button

Personalization
Change desktop background | Change the color scheme
Adjust screen resolution | Change screen saver | Change the theme

Personalization

3. With the default Control Panel category view, select Appearance and Personalization and then select the Personalization option

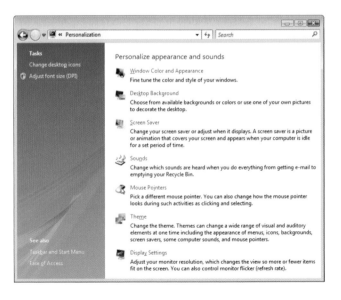

170

See page 11 for the specifications of Windows Vista capable PCs and Windows Premium ready PCs.

The options that each of these enable depend on the edition of Windows Vista that you have installed on your computer, the features available (in particular the processor and the amounts of system memory and graphics memory) and your display settings. Taken together, these dictate which visual schemes (Windows Classic, Windows Vista Basic and Windows Aero) can be used.

1 Open Personalization and select the Windows Color and Appearance option

Beware

The Windows Color option is displayed for the Windows Aero scheme only. The Classic and Vista Basic schemes, have just the Appearance Settings dialog shown below.

2 With the Windows Aero color scheme active, the color selection is displayed

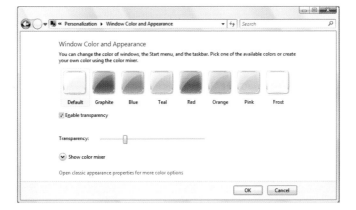

Don't forget

You can adjust the level of transparency, and you can also create a custom color using the sliders in the color mixer.

171

3 Choose one of the predefined colors to change the color for windows, the Start menu and the taskbar

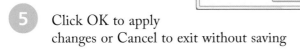

4 Click the Open classic appearance properties, to show the Appearance Settings dialog box

5 Click OK to apply changes or Cancel to exit without saving

Desktop Icons

There are several system icons that may be displayed on the desktop, and the programs that you install may also add icons to the desktop. You can control the display of these icons:

1 Right-click the desktop, click View and click Show Desktop Icons. A check mark is added

2 To remove the check mark, right-click the desktop, click View and click Show Desktop Icons again

3 To resize the icons, right-click the desktop, click View and click Large Icons, Medium Icons or Small Icons

If you have a high resolution screen, you may find that the icons and text are too small. There are two ways to increase their sizes.

1 Reduce the screen resolution. Right-click the desktop, click Personalize, Display settings and drag the slider

Don't forget

At 1600x1200 there are almost 2 million pixels available to render the screen. At 800x600, there are less than half a million, so the results will appear somewhat fuzzy.

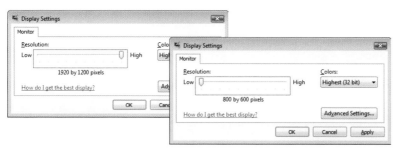

Icons and text will look larger on the screen. However, they are rendered using fewer pixels.

To increase the sizes without giving up pixels:

1 Right click the desktop, select the Personalize entry, then click the option to Adjust Font Size (DPI)

2 Choose 120 DPI (125%) or a custom value, for example 192 DPI (200%)

Hot tip

The text and icons in application windows will similarly increase in size without losing pixels.

The icons and text are increased in size without sacrificing the sharpness of the displayed text, icons and images.

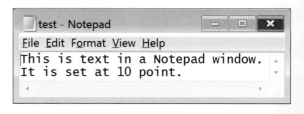

Desktop Background

1 Open Personalization and select Desktop Background to apply a color or to display a picture on the desktop

Hot tip

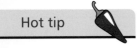

These options are available, whichever color scheme is in effect. See page 175 for examples with Vista Basic and with Aero.

2 Choose a Windows wallpaper from those supplied. Some of the pictures are designed for wide screen displays

Don't forget

The image you choose may be stretched to fit the screen, tiled or centered on the screen, as you wish.

3 Click the Picture Location box to choose an image from one of the picture folders or, click the Browse button to search for an image file

4 Click Solid Colors to select a plain background for the desktop

The results of the personalization will depend on which color scheme is enabled on your computer. If you have Windows Aero, the desktop and windows will exhibit the features that it offers:

Transparent Sidebar

Transparent Icons

Transparent Titlebar

Transparent Frame

Live Taskbar
(see also page 177)

If you have Windows Vista Basic enabled, the same setup will show less striking visual effects and only limited transparency.

Transparent Sidebar

Transparent Icons

Opaque Titlebar

Opaque Frame

Passive Taskbar

Windows Flip and Flip 3D

With several windows open, you can switch between them with the Alt+Tab key, known as Windows Flip. The form this takes depends on the color scheme (see page 41).

Windows Vista Basic

Windows Aero

However, Windows Vista also supports Flip 3D to switch windows, with the Windows Logo key + Tab.

1. Press and hold WinKey+Tab to open Flip 3D, then press Tab repeatedly, or rotate the mouse wheel, to cycle through the windows. Release WinKey to display the window at the front of the stack

Live Window Previews

When you move the mouse pointer over a taskbar button:

Windows Vista Basic shows the window title for the task, or the number of windows for grouped tasks (see page 96).

With Windows Aero, you see a live thumbnail sized preview of the window contents or the contents of the first window for grouped tasks.

This works for all types of windows. For example, if one of the windows has video or animation, this will play in the preview.

This works for all types of windows. For example, if one of the windows has video or animation, this will play in the preview.

Select a grouped task

If there are a group of tasks, click the associated taskbar button to show the list of tasks by window title. With Windows Aero, holding the mouse pointer over a particular entry will display a live thumbnail preview, as described above.

If you'd prefer not to group your tasks:

 Right-click the taskbar and select Properties then Clear the box labeled Group similar taskbar buttons

☑ Group similar taskbar buttons

☑ Show Quick Launch

☑ Show window previews

Don't forget

Clear the box marked Show window previews (as shown at Step 1 below), to switch off the live windows previews in Windows Aero.

177

Hot tip

See page 180 for more information about the taskbar properties.

Screen Saver

When your mouse or keyboard has been idle for a specified period of time, Windows will display a moving image or pattern known as a screen saver. To specify the image used:

1 From Personalization, select Screen Saver, then choose a screen saver from the list, for example, Photos

2 Set the time delay after which the screen saver will be invoked, and choose to display the logon screen when the system resumes

3 Click the Preview button to check out the action. Click OK to put the screen saver or settings into effect

Note that some screen savers and some special features (e.g. Themes on the Photos screen saver) will only be available if you have a sufficiently powerful graphics adapter installed on your computer.

The screen saver can't run because it requires a newer video card or one that's compatible with Direct3D.

Sounds

1 Select Sounds from Personalization, to see the sound theme that gets applied to events in Windows

Hot tip

If you do not want to have sounds associated with Windows events, select No Sounds.

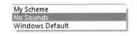

2 Select an event such as Windows Logoff and click the Test button to hear the associated sound

3 Browse to locate a new sound file (file type .wav), then click Test to preview the effect

4 Make any other changes, then click Save As, and provide a name for your modified sound scheme

Taskbar

180

Don't forget

You can customize the Taskbar so that it is automatically hidden when you are not using it. You can also lock it to prevent accidental resizing or moving, or unlock to make changes.

Hot tip

If the Taskbar is already locked (see tick symbol), clicking the entry will unlock the taskbar.

✓ Lock the Taskbar

Hot tip

You can also drag the Taskbar to the right or left edge of the screen.

① Right-click an empty part of the Taskbar

② Click Toolbars to add or remove specific toolbars

③ Click Lock the Taskbar to lock the Taskbar

④ Select Properties from the Taskbar menu, and select Auto-hide the Taskbar

⑤ The Taskbar is hidden, but reappears when you move the mouse pointer over its position

⑥ Unlock the Taskbar, then click an empty part of the Taskbar and drag it to the top edge of the desktop

⑦ Also with the Taskbar unlocked, point to the edge of the Taskbar. When the pointer becomes a double-headed arrow, drag it up or down, to adjust the Taskbar size

Desktop Themes

The desktop theme allows you to apply a set of related changes, affecting the style of windows, menus, icons, fonts, colors, sounds and mouse pointers. To view the themes available:

1. Open Personalization and select Theme, to display the Theme Settings dialog box

Don't forget

Several themes are included in Windows, but you can search for more themes online, or you can buy them in theme packs at a computer store. You must install a theme in order to see it in the list of available themes.

2. Select a theme, e.g. Windows Classic, to view its color and style

3. Click OK to accept the selected theme and apply it to your system

Windows Sidebar

Windows Sidebar, briefly introduced on page 22, is a vertical bar displayed on the side of your desktop. It contains small programs known as Gadgets, which offer information or provide easy access to frequently used tools. The gadgets installed by default are:

introduced on page 22

Clock (any time zone)

Slide Show (pictures)

News Headlines

To see what other gadgets are available:

1   At the top of Sidebar, click the plus sign (+) to open the Gadget Gallery

2   Click a gadget and then click Show details to see information about it at the bottom of the dialog box

CPU Meter 1.0.0.0
See the current computer CPU and system memory (RAM).

Microsoft Corporation
© 2006
Windows www.microsoftgadgets.com

To add a gadget to Windows Sidebar:

1   Right-click the new gadget in the Gadget Gallery and select Add

Gadget Gallery

You can download additional gadgets from the Microsoft Gallery:

1 Open the Gadget Gallery (see page 182) and click the link Get more gadgets online

2 The sidebar gadgets available are listed so you can select a category, or search by keyword

Open the Gadget Gallery (see page 182)

Don't forget

The gadgets are submitted by individuals, so the ones that are on offer will change from time to time.

183

Beware

Some of the gadgets will be Web Gadgets for use online with Windows Live, rather than Sidebar Gadgets.

3 Locate a gadget that interests you and click the Download button, and choose to Save the file to hard disk

4 Run the downloaded file to install the gadget on the Sidebar and in the Gadget Gallery

User Accounts

If more than one person uses the computer, each person can have a user account defined by a user name and optional password. There are three different types of accounts:

- Standard Account – this is the account to use for everyday computing. It lets you use most programs that are installed on the computer, but you can't install or uninstall software and hardware, delete files that are required for the computer to work or change settings on the computer that affect other users

- Administrator Account – this provides the most control over the computer, and should only be used when necessary, e.g. to carry out activities not permitted for a standard user account

- Guest Account – this is primarily for people who need temporary access to the computer. People using the guest account can't install software or hardware, change settings or create a password

Create a user account

User Accounts and Family Safety
Set up parental controls for any user
Add or remove user accounts

1 Select Control Panel, then Add or Remove User Accounts (under User Accounts and Family Safety)

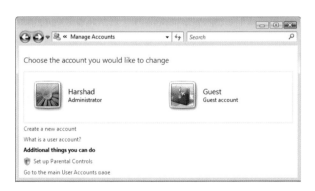

2 Click Create a new account

3 Type the name you want to give the user account, click an account type and then click Create Account

Strong Passwords

You should make sure you have strong passwords for all accounts on your computer.

Switch User Accounts

The ability to switch to a different user account without logging off or closing programs and files is called Fast User Switching. To switch to a different user account, follow these steps:

1 Click the Start button, click the arrow next to the Lock button and then click Switch User

2 Select the new user name from the Welcome screen

Change the User Name Picture

1 Select Add or Remove User Accounts (see previous page), choose your account and click Change the picture

2 Select a new picture for the account

Date and Time Functions

To change the format Windows uses to display dates and times:

1 Select Control Panel, click Clock Language and Region, and then click Regional and Language Options

 **Clock, Language, and Region**
Change keyboards or other input methods
Change display language

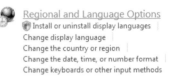 **Regional and Language Options**
Install or uninstall display languages
Change display language
Change the country or region
Change the date, time, or number format
Change keyboards or other input methods

2 The Format tab shows how various data items are displayed

186

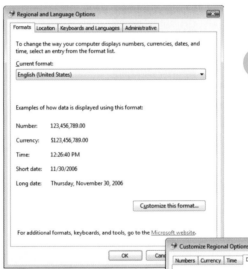

3 Select a different locale, e.g. United Kingdom or Australia, if appropriate

4 Click the Date tab to make changes to the way that dates are shown

5 Click the Time tab to change the way that times are displayed

Windows Calendar lets you plan and manage your activities, create a personal task list, coordinate your schedule with others, and receive automatic notifications and reminders about specific tasks and upcoming appointments.

1 Select Start, All Programs, Windows Calendar

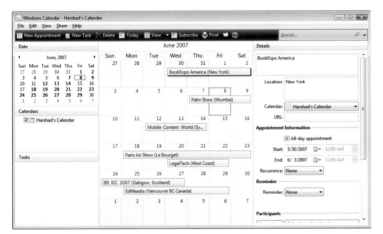

Hot tip

Click Print on the toolbar, or select File, Print menu tool. You can print your calendar, by day, work week, calendar week or month.

187

2 Click View and choose to view your calendar by day, work week, calendar week or month

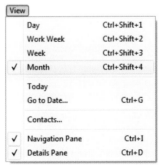

3 You can display or hide the Navigation Pane and the Details Pane

Windows Calendar Functions

The Windows Calendar can provide full diary management functions, including:

- **Add** appointments

- Invite attendees to meetings

- Create and prioritize tasks

- Subscribe to online calendars

- Publish to the Internet

Don't forget

Windows Calendar lets you add all types of appointments, including all day events and recurring appointments, and has a reminder feature so you won't forget a task or a meeting.

Windows Media Player Skins

Give Windows Media Player a new look by applying a skin.

1 Select Start, All Programs, Windows Media Player

2 If the Menu bar is hidden, press Alt and select View, Skin Chooser

3 If the Menu bar is visible, select View, Skin Chooser

4 Select the skin that you want to apply. A preview appears

5 Click Apply Skin. This displays the Player in skin mode using the skin that you chose

Click Minimize to display the miniplayer on the taskbar

Ultimate Extras

Windows Ultimate Extras are features that are exclusive to users of Windows Vista Ultimate edition. They are not included with the installation package but can be downloaded via Windows Update (see page 225). They are add-ons to extend the capabilities of your operating system or just make your PC more fun to use. The Extras currently available include:

- Windows DreamScene
- Windows Hold'em Poker Game
- BitLocker Drive Preparation Tool
- Secure Online Key Backup

Whenever a new Ultimate Extra is ready for distribution, you will see the Ultimate Extra control panel informing you that there are new extras to download and install.

To check what's currently available:

1 Select Start, All Programs, Extras and Upgrades, select Windows Ultimate Extras and click View Available Extras

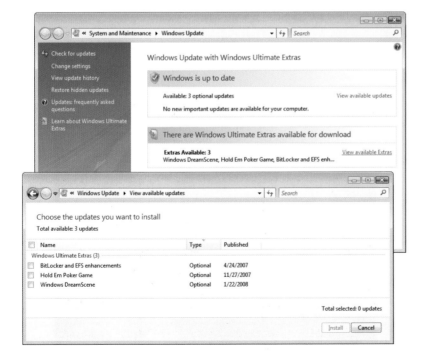

Don't forget

Microsoft has announced plans to release new Ultimate Extras, including enhancements to Movie Maker and DVD Maker, new DreamScene videos, screen savers and sound schemes.

Beware

Vista Ultimate had an entry for the Ultimate Extras on the Welcome Center but they were removed in the SP1 update (see page 227).

Hot tip

Click the boxes to indicate which Extras you wish to add to your system, then click the Install button.

Windows DreamScene

Windows DreamScene supports animated video wallpaper and allows you to use and run high-resolution and high-definition video contents as your desktop background, as part of the Windows Vista Aero Glass user interface.

 Open Personalization, select Desktop Background and choose the Windows DreamScene Content entry

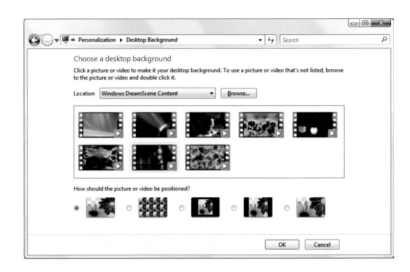

 Choose a video and click OK to apply it to the desktop, then close the personalization window

BitLocker Tools

BitLocker helps protect you from the risks of data theft and disclosure, by preventing access to files stored on the protected drive. It makes use of Trusted Platform Module (TMP) hardware if included in your system, or you can use a USB memory key. It incorporates drive encryption and integrity checking of early boot components to ensure that the system hasn't been tampered with.

Detailed guidance is provided for setting up your system, but the two Ultimate Extras make it much easier to manage.

1 Click Start, All Programs, Accessories, System Tools, BitLocker and select BitLocker Drive Preparation Tool

2 Click Continue to partition your drive, creating a separate system drive (S:) for the Boot components, and follow the steps to encrypt the rest of your disk

3 Click Start, All Programs, Extras and Upgrades and select Secure Online Key Backup

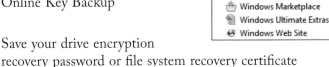

4 Save your drive encryption recovery password or file system recovery certificate

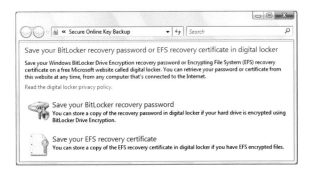

Don't forget

The BitLocker Drive Encryption feature is available in the Ultimate and Enterprise editions of Windows Vista.

Hot tip

Select the BitLocker Drive Preparation Tool Readme in the BitLocker folder for a description of the tool and for pointers to other sources of information.

191

Don't forget

The recovery information will be stored in a free Microsoft website known as the Digital Locker.

More Information

1 For more information about Ultimate Extras, visit website http://www.ultimatepc.com and click Extras & Exclusives

2 You'll find useful insights from Windows Vista Team at website http://windowsvistablog.com/blogs/windowsvista

3 The website http:/www.windowsvistamagazine.com/ offers help and advice from other Vista users

12 Digital Media

Windows Vista makes it very easy to work with digital media, with a variety of tools to organize your collections of pictures, videos and music files, create your own CDs and DVDs, and use your PC as an interactive media center.

Upload Pictures

Windows makes it easy to transfer pictures from digital media, camera or scanner. Here's an example using a media card reader.

 Plug the reader into a USB port on the computer

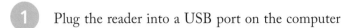 The Found New Hardware Wizard will start the first time to help you install the software for your device from the manufacturer's CD or from the Internet

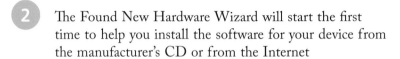 The device software is installed with a drive letter automatically assigned to your device

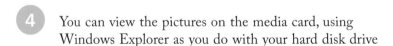 You can view the pictures on the media card, using Windows Explorer as you do with your hard disk drive

Pictures Folder

Each user account has a personal Pictures folder.

1. Open the Pictures folder from the folder list on the right of the Start menu, from Windows Explorer or from the navigation pane (see page 38) in any folder

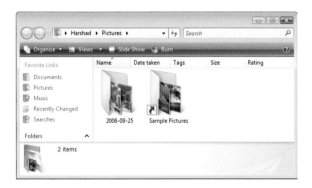

Hot tip

This is a convenient place to store and organize digital images, especially as graphic design and photo-edit programs assume this as the default location.

2. Double-click a folder to display its contents

Hot tip

The contents of the Command bar change when a file is selected, adding options relevant to the type of item, e.g. Preview, Print and Share, for an image file.

195

3. To use a picture as your desktop wallpaper, right-click the image icon and select Set as Desktop Background

4. This menu also offers the options to rotate the image, useful when you have taken a photograph in portrait mode

Don't forget

The pictures in the folder are displayed as large icons (thumbnails), but you can change this with the Views options (see page 59).

Windows Photo Gallery

Beware

Deleting a picture from the Gallery will delete it from the containing folder and remove it from your computer.

1 Connect your digital camera or media card reader. Windows will detect the picture files and offer suitable actions

2 Select Import pictures using Windows

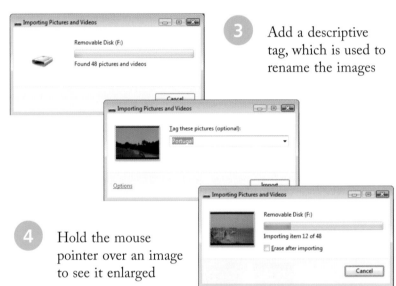

3 Add a descriptive tag, which is used to rename the images

4 Hold the mouse pointer over an image to see it enlarged

Hot tip

Windows detects your newest pictures, and does not import duplicates of pictures that you have previously copied to your computer.

Hot tip

The files on the camera or media card are copied to a subfolder in the Pictures folder. Windows Photo Gallery opens with Recently Imported selected.

To specify which images Windows Photo Gallery will display:

1 Select Pictures to show all the image files in the Gallery

2 Select a Tag (keyword) associated with a set of images. You can add one or more tags to any picture or group of pictures

3 Display all pictures taken in a specific period (year, month or particular day)

4 Display images by ratings (you can associate a value of up to five stars to any image or selection of images)

5 Double-click an image file to see it full size

6 The zoom, slide show and rotation controls are activated

Don't forget

Windows Photo Gallery allows you to view and organize all the pictures stored in your Pictures folder and subfolders, the public Pictures, and any other image folders you add to the Gallery.

197

Don't forget

Click Fix to Auto Adjust your photos, or to apply the changes individually, adjusting brightness, contrast, color and size, and removing red eye effects.

Windows Movie Maker

You use Windows Movie Maker to obtain audio and video clips from a digital video camera, then use this captured content in your movies. You can also import existing audio, video or still pictures into Windows Movie Maker to incorporate in the movies.

Don't forget

Windows Movie Maker is included in the Home Premium and the Ultimate editions of Windows Vista.

1 Select Start, All Programs, and click Windows Movie Maker

2 Movie Maker warns you if there are problems with your graphics card support for required features e.g. DirectX9

3 Click the Import Media button to select your video clips and then click the Import button

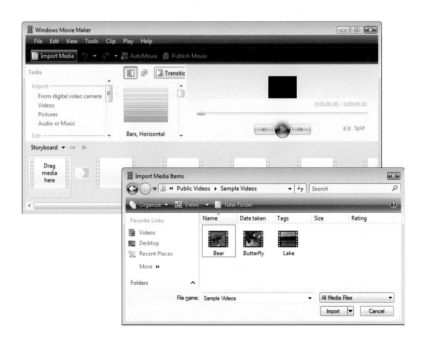

Hot tip

You can use Windows Photo Gallery (see page 196) to organize and manage your video clips.

4 Drag and drop the video clips to assemble the parts of your movie on the storyboard for your current project

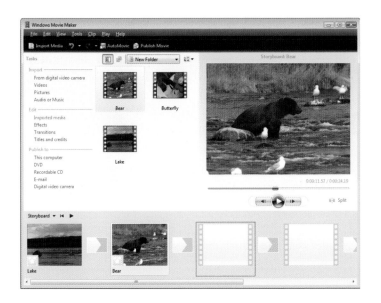

Hot tip

Drag clips, transitions, or effects to the storyboard or the timeline for your current project. You can also drag clips to the preview monitor to play them there.

5 Select View and click Timeline or Storyboard (or press Ctrl+T which acts as a toggle between the two)

Hot tip

After editing the audio and video content in Windows Movie Maker, adding titles and video transitions, you can save your movie and share it with your friends and family.

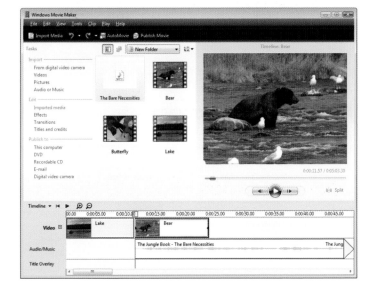

6 You can add sound tracks, titles and transition effects

Windows DVD Maker

Don't forget

There's no need to select an AutoPlay action when you insert the blank DVD - just click the [x] to close the window.

You can create DVD-Video discs using Windows DVD Maker, adding video, pictures and audio to make slide shows. You can also add projects created using Movie Maker. The discs run in a DVD player so you can watch your movies and slide shows on your TV. To create a DVD:

1 Insert a blank DVD into your DVD writer

2 Select Start, All Programs, then click Windows DVD Maker

3 The first time, you'll see an initial welcome screen. Make sure that the Don't show this Page Again box is ticked

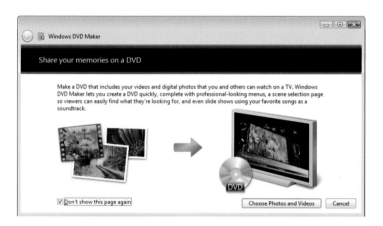

4 Click Choose Pictures and Videos to open the project

Hot tip

By default, Windows DVD Maker will enter the current date as the disc title for the project, but you can append this or enter a new title.

5 Specify the disc title then click the Add Items button

6 Choose the photographs and video clips that you require

7 When you've added all the items, click Next

8 Click the Burn button to write the project to the DVD

Windows Media Player

The Windows Media Player will manage audio and video digital media files, allowing you to copy music files, organize your collections, download media files etc.

Hot tip

If the box labeled Always do this for audio CDs is ticked, then the next time that you insert an audio CD, your selected action will be applied automatically.

Don't forget

To open Windows Media Player without inserting a CD, select Start, All Programs, Windows Media Player.

Hot tip

The next time you insert this CD, the album details will be displayed without having to connect to the Internet.

 To play an audio CD, Insert the disc into the CD drive

If the autoplay option isn't already set, click Play audio CD using Windows Media Player

Windows Media Player starts up and begins playing the CD from track one

 If you are connected to the Internet, the artist, album title and track details are automatically downloaded

To skip a track, click the Next button. To always skip such tracks, click the album title and select Skip During Playback

Copy Audio CD

You can rip (copy) tracks from your audio CDs, so that they are stored as digital files, based on the settings.

1. Click the Rip tab button, then click the arrow below Rip, and select More Options

2. Choose the location to store files

3. Select the format, e.g. .wma, .mp3 or .wav

4. Specify the quality that you require

5. Click OK then click the Start Rip button

Hot tip

By default, the files will be stored as a subfolder within the user's own Music folder.

Beware

Copy protection is available for Windows Media Audio (.wma) format. However, if you intend to use the digital audio files on more than one computer, do not copy protect the files.

203

6. The album is added to the Music folder

Play DVD Movies

Don't forget

To play DVDs you must have a DVD drive and a compatible DVD decoder, such as provided on systems that include Windows Media Center (see page 207).

Hot tip

If Media Player is already running, click the arrow below Now Playing, and click the DVD drive to start the movie.

1 To play a DVD movie, insert the disc into the drive

2 If autoplay isn't set, click Play DVD movie using Windows Media Player

3 Windows Media Player starts up and begins playing the movie, initially in full screen mode

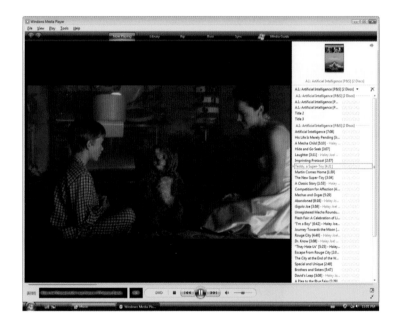

4 To switch between full screen and windowed display, press the toggle key combination Alt+Enter

5 Press the DVD button and select Special Features, to access the extra items on the disc

Media Library

Windows Media Player monitors your personal folders and adds information about the music, video and picture files that they contain or that you add. When you play CDs, the downloaded information about the discs is also added. When you play a digital file on your computer or on the internet, those details are also added, if not already in the library.

Beware

The Media Player does not automatically add files that you play from removable storage or network drives.

1 To display the library, start the Media Player and click the Library tab button

2 The library displays the category that you viewed last, in this case Music. View the contents by artist, album etc.

3 To display a different category, click the Select a Category button, and choose from the list offered

Don't forget

The library contains links to the digital media files on your computer, it does not have actual copies of the files. These are contained in the Music, Videos and Pictures folders.

4 To remove an entry from the library, right-click it and select Delete. You'll be asked if you want to remove just the library link or to remove the file completely

Online Resources

1 To browse the stores, click the arrow below the Online Stores tab button and then click Browse all Online Stores

2 To view an electronic magazine, select Media Guide

3 To listen to online radio, select the Internet Radio link

Windows Media Center

Vista Home Premium and Ultimate editions offer another way to manage digital media files and play CDs and DVDs, and in addition support TV and FM Radio. To explore this feature:

1 Select Start, All Programs, Windows Media Center. The first time you do this, you must run the setup program

2 You can choose to periodically connect to the Internet to download cover art and music, movie and TV guides

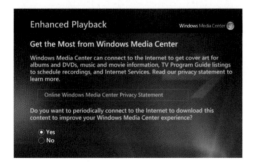

3 When configuration completes, scroll to the Music section to begin cataloging your multimedia files

Hot tip

Select Express Setup and you are enrolled in the customer feedback program. Select Custom setup to make your own choices.

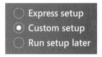

Beware

The configuration options offered depend on the multimedia hardware available on your machine.

...cont'd

4 Windows Media Center will locate and identify your music files and set up your music library

5 Scroll to the Online Media section to explore its options, which include TV, movies, music, news and sport

6 For example, select the Showcase option and select Arsenal TV to watch games or view greatest moments etc

Reference section: Maintenance

Windows includes a set of tools to enhance the security, performance and reliability of your PC. It helps you to maintain your hard drive at peak efficiency, configure your power options and manage your system when you make hardware and software changes. It protects your computer from malicious software and keeps your system up to date.

System Properties

There are several ways to open the System Properties, and view information about your computer:

1 Double-click the View Computer Details item in the Welcome Center

2 Select Start, Control Panel, System and Maintenance, then click System

System and Maintenance
Get started with Windows
Back up your computer

System
View amount of RAM and processor speed
Check your computer's Windows Experience Index base score
Allow remote access   See the name of this computer

Open
Explore
Manage
Map Network Drive
Create Shortcut
Delete
Rename
Properties

3 Press the Windows Logo + the Pause/Break keys

4 Right-click Computer on the desktop (or on the Start menu) and choose Properties

Device Manager

1 Click Device Manager, to list all of the hardware components installed on your computer

2 Click the [+] to expand that entry

3 Click the [-] to collapse the expanded entry

4 Double-click any device to open its properties

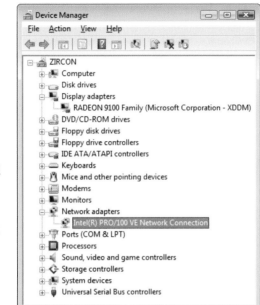

5 Select the Drivers tab and click Update Driver to install new software

6 Select Disable to put the particular device offline

Don't forget

You will be prompted for an administrator password or asked for permission to continue, when you select the Device Manager entry.

211

Hot tip

Click the Roll Back Driver button to switch back to the previously installed driver for that device, if the new one fails.

Performance Information

Performance Information and Tools displays your computer's Windows Experience Index, which helps establish the overall capability of your system. To view the details:

1   Open System Properties and click Performance. For a Vista Capable PC:

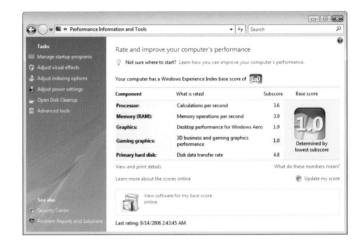

2   The results for a Vista Premium Ready PC are:

3   If you upgrade any of the hardware components on your computer click Update My Score to see the effect

Clean Up Your Disk

1 Open Performance Information and Tools and click Start Disk Cleanup

2 Choose whether to deal with your files only or files for all users

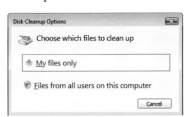

3 Select the drive letter, if there's more than one drive available

4 Drive Cleanup scans the drive to identify files that can be safely removed

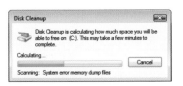

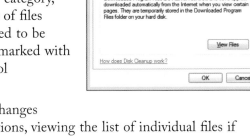

5 All the possible files are listed by category, and the sets of files recommended to be deleted are marked with a tick symbol

6 Make any changes to the selections, viewing the list of individual files if necessary to help you choose, then click OK

7 Deleted files won't be transferred to the Recycle Bin, so confirm that you do want to permanently delete all of these files, and the disk space will be made available

Hot tip

You can select Start, All Programs, Accessories, System Tools, Disk Cleanup. You can also select Start, type Disk Cleanup and select the program from the top of the Start menu.

Don't forget

You can have more than one hard disk on your computer, or you can divide one hard disk into several partitions, with separate drive letters.

213

Beware

You can select any of the groups of files listed, but this could affect the operation of some functions, for example, hibernate.

...cont'd

When a file is written to the hard disk, it may be stored in several pieces at different positions. This fragmentation of the disk space can slow down your computer. Disk Defragmenter will rearrange the fragmented data so the disk works more efficiently.

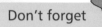
Don't forget

Click Start, All Programs, Accessories, System Tools to locate the Disk Defragmenter program.

1 Select Start, type Disk Defrag and click the Disk Defragmenter at the top of the Start menu

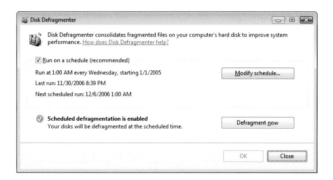

Don't forget

This is another program which prompts for an administrator password or asks for permission to continue.

2 The program runs as a scheduled task (see page 215) but you can click Defragment Now to run it immediately

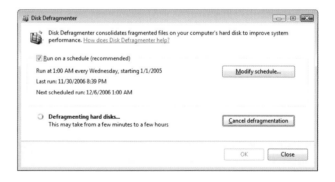

Hot tip

Advanced users can use the command line tool Defrag.exe to analyze only, to generate detailed reports and to process multiple volumes.

Disk Defragmenter may take from several minutes to several hours to complete, depending on the size of the disk and the amount of fragmentation present, but you can still use your computer while the task is taking place, or you can press Cancel Defragmentation, and continue the process at another time, perhaps using the task scheduler.

Schedule Tasks

If there is a program that you use on a regular basis, run the Task Scheduler Wizard to create a task that will open the application on the appropriate dates and at the required time.

Hot tip

The Scheduler can be used for any type of program, not just systems maintenance programs like Disk Cleanup and Disk Defragmenter.

1. Select Start, All Programs, Accessories, System Tools, then click the Task Scheduler entry

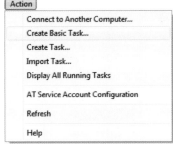

2. Select Action, Create Basic Task

3. Provide a name for the task, and an optional description

Don't forget

You can schedule tasks based on the calendar (e.g. daily or weekly) or on commonly occurring events such as when the computer starts or when you log on.

4. Follow the prompts to choose a schedule (e.g. daily at 11am), and specify the action (e.g. start a program)

5. The task will be added to the list and carried out according to your instructions

Configure Power Options

1 Select Start, Control Panel, Hardware and Sound and then select Power Options, or

Hardware and Sound
Printer
Mouse

Power Options
Change power-saving settings
Change what the power buttons do
Require a password when the computer wakes
Change when the computer sleeps

in the Classic view, double-click Power Options

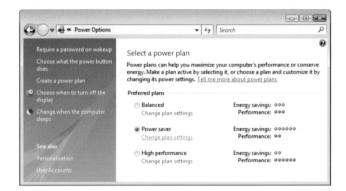

2 Select a power plan, and click Change plan settings

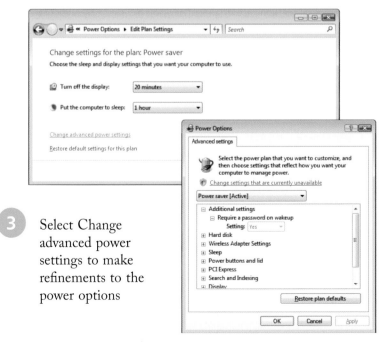

3 Select Change advanced power settings to make refinements to the power options

Back Up and Recover Data

To make sure you don't lose the files that you create, modify and store on your computer, you should back them up regularly. You can manually back up your files, or set up automatic backups.

1 Click Back up your computer, in Control Panel, to open Back Up and Restore Center

System and Maintenance
Get started with Windows
Back up your computer

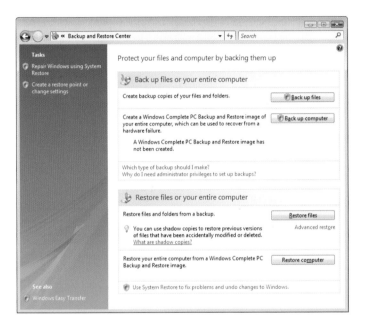

Beware

The ability to set up automatic backups is not included in Windows Vista Starter and Windows Vista Home Basic editions.

Don't forget

Create a complete backup of your entire computer disk, when you first set up your computer. Then backup your data files on a regular basis.

217

2 Click Back up files, then follow the wizard prompts to specify where to store the data and which type of files to backup

3 Similarly, click Restore Files, when you want to recover files. Again, you'll be guided through the process

Store the media used for backups (external hard disks, DVDs or CDs) in a secure place. A separate fireproof location is the ideal.

Hot tip

As with most system related tasks, you may be prompted for an administrator password or asked for permission to continue.

Windows Easy Transfer

You can transfer files and settings from one Windows computer to another, including documents and pictures, email information, user accounts and settings, Internet connection settings and favorites, music files and playlists.

1 Start Windows Easy Transfer on the old computer, from the System Tools subfolder in the Start menu

Hot tip

You can also transfer files and settings from a Windows 2000 or Windows XP computer, by following prompts to copy Windows Easy Transfer from your Windows Vista system.

2 Follow the prompts to start a new transfer, and choose the method of transfer to be used

Don't forget

You can use an Easy Transfer Cable (USB to USB), your home network, a USB flash drive, an external hard disk, DVDs or CDs, but floppy disks transfers are not supported.

3 You can transfer everything from all users or from your user account only, or you can make a custom selection

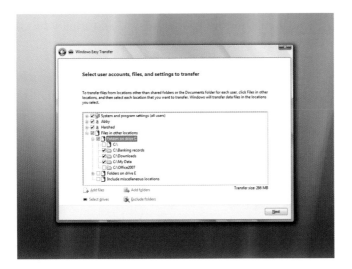

219

Beware

During this process, you will not be able to use either computer. Make sure you have pre-installed all required programs on your new computer before you start the transfer.

4 The files and settings will be transferred, using the method you selected

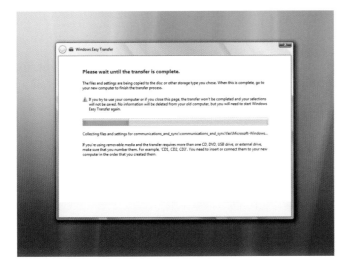

Don't forget

Insert the removable media (e.g. DVD or CD) into your new computer.

5 Run Windows Easy Transfer on your new computer, to copy the files and apply the settings

System Restore

System Restore
returns system files
to an earlier point in
time, allowing you to
undo system changes
without affecting your
documents, email, and
other data files.

The installation of a new program or driver software may make
Windows behave unpredictably or have other unexpected results.
Usually, uninstalling the program or rolling back the driver
(see page 211) will correct the situation. If this does not fix the
problem, you should restore your system to an earlier date when
everything worked correctly.

 Select Start, All Programs, Accessories, System tools and
then select System Restore. By default this will offer to
undo the most recent change. This may fix the problem

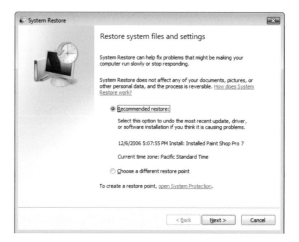

Don't forget

You can also run System
Restore from Safe Mode,
the troubleshooting
option. Start up the
computer and press
F8 repeatedly as your
computer reboots, to
display the boot menu,
then select Safe Mode.

Otherwise, click Choose a different restore point, for
example, to a time before the problem was first observed

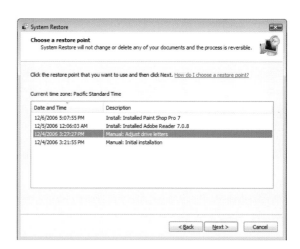

Create a restore point

If you are making a change to your system, hardware or software, take a snapshot of the system beforehand.

1 Start System Restore and click Open System Protection

2 Click the Create button, to create a restore point manually

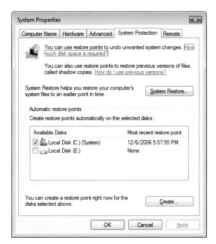

3 Provide a title for the restore point and click Create

4 The required data is written to disk and the restore point is set up

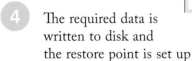

Hot tip

You can specify which drive to store the automatic or manual restore points, if you have more than one hard disk.

Beware

System Restore is not intended for personal data files. For these you should use the file backup program (see page 217).

221

Windows Security Center

Windows Security Center helps to keep your system safe by checking the status of security programs on your computer. If Windows detects a problem with any of these (for example, if your antivirus program is out of date) Security Center displays a message and places a Security Center icon in the notification area.

1. Double-click the Security Center icon to open Security Center and review the status of your security settings

2. You can also open Security Center from the Control Panel, in standard or in classic view

Security
Check for updates
Check this computer's security status
Allow a program through Windows Firewall

Security Center

222

3. Security items marked On or OK are colored green. Items with messages are amber (warning) or red

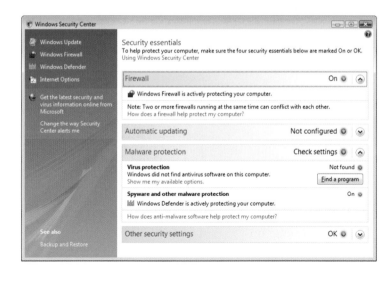

4. Click the ⊙ arrow buttons to expand the item and display the messages. Click the ⊙ arrow to collapse the item

Windows Firewall

1 Open Windows Firewall from the Control Panel, in standard or in classic view

Windows Firewall
Turn Windows Firewall on or off
Allow a program through Windows Firewal

Windows
Firewall

Hot tip

You can also click Windows Firewall in the links in Security Center.

Windows Security Center

Windows Update

Windows Firewall

2 Click Turn Windows Firewall on or off to reveal the General tab

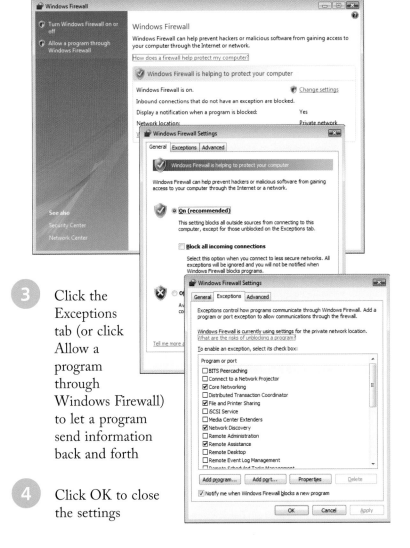

Don't forget

Firewall is on by default in Windows Vista, but you can turn it off if you have another Firewall installed and active. Note that if you have a router with a built in firewall, you still need the Windows Firewall (or other firewall) on your computer.

3 Click the Exceptions tab (or click Allow a program through Windows Firewall) to let a program send information back and forth

4 Click OK to close the settings

Malware Protection

Windows Defender is installed and turned on by default, and will guard against spyware and adware.

Windows Defender
Scan for spyware and other potentially unwanted software

Windows Defender

1 Click Windows Defender in Control Panel, Security (or in Classic view double-click Windows Defender)

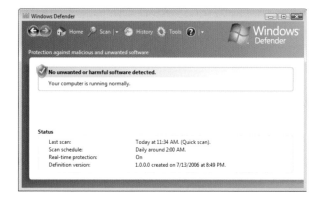

2 Click Tools, then select Options and adjust settings such as automatic scanning and default actions

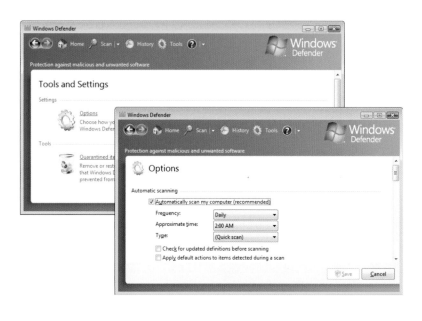

Windows Update

Installing updates to the programs on your computer can prevent
or fix problems, improve the security or enhance performance.
For updates to Windows and its associated programs:

Security
Check for updates
Check this computer's security status
Allow a program through Windows Firewall

Windows
Update

1 Click Check for Updates in Control Panel, Security (or in
Classic view double-click Windows Update)

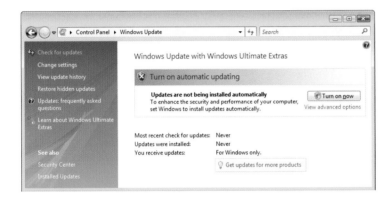

2 If Windows Update is currently not configured, click the
button Turn on now. Otherwise click Check for updates

3 The updates will be automatically installed. If updates are
turned off, click the button Install updates

Hot tip

Alternatively, you can
click Windows Update
from Security Center.

Don't forget

You can get updates
for Microsoft Office
and other Microsoft
programs, as well as
Windows, if you click
Get updates for more
products, and enable
Microsoft Update.

Beware

If you have a dial-up
line, you should change
the settings, so you can
control when updates
are downloaded.

Change Settings

 **1** Open Windows Update and click Change settings

 **2** The recommended option is to install updates automatically. This assumes a broadband link

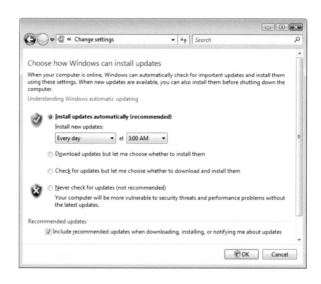

3 You can specify to download updates in the background, but pick your own time to install them

4 Windows Update will check for updates, but leave you to decide when to download and install them

5 The final option offered is to turn off Windows Update and never check for updates. You may wish to do this when you are traveling where the Internet connections available are unsuitable for downloading

Overview of SP1

For a detailed description of the Windows Vista Service Pack 1:

1　Visit website http://technet.microsoft.com/windowsvista/ and click the Service Pack tab

Although there's a multitude of changes contained in SP1, you'll find that the changes are very much fine tuning, under-the-cover affairs. They fit into three main categories:

1: Quality Improvements

- **Application and Device Compatibility:** When Windows Vista launched, there were 13,000 additional components and devices supported by Windows Update. With SP1 there is support for more than 54,000 components and devices

- **Reliability:** Among the improvements, SP1 helps prevent data loss while ejecting NTFS file system–formatted removable media, improves the reliability of networking and extends the Backup program to include encrypted files

- **Performance:** Enhancements include faster browsing of network file shares, improved file copying (40% to 70% quicker), faster adding and extracting files from compressed folders, better power transitions (for example, resuming from hibernation and standby mode). Battery life is improved by reducing CPU use and redrawing the screen less frequently

- **Security:** SP1 improves BitLocker Drive Encryption, adding encryption of all local volumes, not just drive C. There's an additional multifactor authentication method that combines a TPM–protected key with a startup key stored on a USB device and a user-generated PIN

...cont'd

2: Emerging Hardware and Standards

- **New Hardware:** There is enhanced support for 64-bit computers, new storage technologies such as exFAT (a new file system that offers larger file sizes and capacity), high-definition (HD) drives and for the latest version of Direct3D (used for 3D-applications and 3D-games). There are also new capabilities for Windows Media Center

- **New Standards:** SP1 includes support for new cryptographic algorithms, new wired and wireless networking standards, and adds support for the Parental Controls Games Restrictions ratings

3: Infrastructure Optimization

- **Deployment and Support:** SP1 provides help for business and corporate administrators managing Windows Vista and Windows Server 2008 configurations. For example, SP1 adds a new version of the Network Diagnostics tool

To see the Network Diagnostic tool in action:

1 Select Start, Network and Network and Sharing Center

2 If you are experiencing networking problems, click the link Diagnose and Repair and it will identify and fix a range of common issues (or else it reports the problem)

Obtaining SP1

The following options are available for obtaining SP1:

1 Windows Update - This will automatically install SP1 on computers that have Automatic Updates enabled

2 Stand-alone SP1 Package - This contains all the files that are needed to install SP1 on any computer. You may find this on a PC magazine cover disc, or download it from the Microsoft website. Search for "Vista Service Pack 1 Standalone" at http://www.microsoft.com/downloads

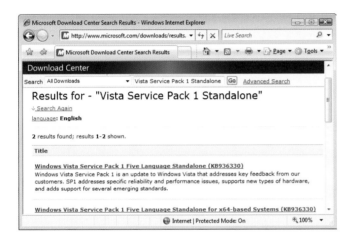

3 Integrated Installation - The service pack is integrated with the operating system on the installation DVD, so SP1 is installed simultaneously with the operating system

4 New Computers - These can be purchased with Vista and SP1 installed

Prerequisite Updates

Computers running the original Windows Vista also require two or three updates before installing SP1. Windows Update will detect your configuration and offer the updates applicable to your system, installing them in sequential order. The updates are:

       KB935509 (Vista Enterprise and Ultimate editions only)
       KB938371
       KB937287

Hot tip

This minimizes the size of the download because only the changes needed for the specific computer are applied. This method is advised for home and small business users.

Hot tip

The download size of the stand-alone package is significantly larger than the package applied with Windows Update, but is effective when updating multiple PCs to SP1.

Hot tip

Use the integrated installation to upgrade computers from Windows XP or for new installations on computers that do not have an operating system.

Don't forget

These updates will be installed prior to SP1 when you use Windows Update. The stand-alone SP1 package includes these updates and applies them first.

Postponing SP1

Don't forget

You could turn off Windows Update (see page 225) but this would also prevent other updates from being installed.

You may want to postpone applying SP1, perhaps to choose a more convenient date and time. Use the SP Blocker tool for this.

1 Visit the Service Pack web page (see page 227) and click the link Windows Service Pack Blocker Tool

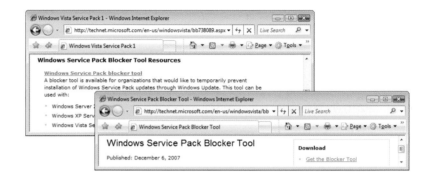

2 Click the link Get the Blocker Tool, then click the Download button and Save the SPBlockerTools.exe program

Download

Run the downloaded program and follow the prompts to extract the program and scripts and save them in a specified folder.

Don't forget

You must open the command prompt with Administrator authority to run this command.

3 Run SPBlockingTool.exe with the option /B (for blocking)

4 To view the Registry entry, select Start, type RegEdit, press Enter and navigate to the WindowsUpdate key

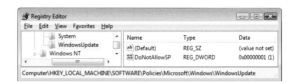

Installing SP1

When SP1 was added to Windows Update it was flagged as an optional update for the first month, becoming an automatic update after that (unless you'd run the SP Blocking tool or turned off automatic updates). To manually invoke the SP1 installation:

1 Open Windows Update and select Install Updates to start the download and installation of SP1

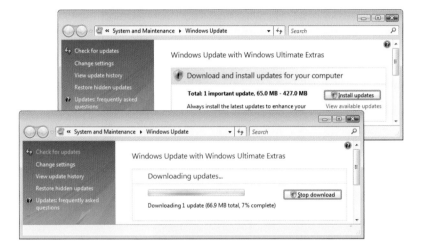

2 When the download completes and installation begins, respond to the initial prompts and close any active tasks

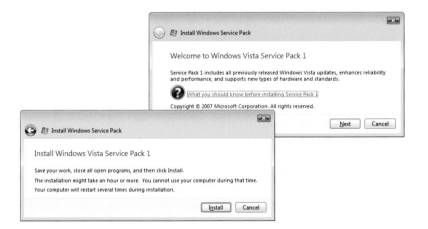

3 The process proceeds without any further interaction

...cont'd

4 The system may restart several times, and you are kept informed by messages and progress indicators displayed during the startup and shutdown stages, in the Vista style

5 There are a variety of messages that might be displayed

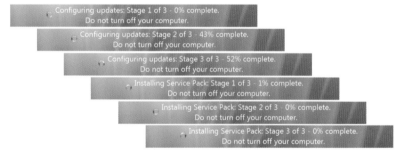

6 When the process completes, settings are personalized and the "Installation was successful" message is displayed

Index

G

H

I

239

X

Y

Z